BOB DYLAN
UKULELE CHORD SONGBOOK

100 classics
with full lyrics and
easy-to-read
ukulele chord boxes

Wise Publications
part of The Music Sales Group
London / New York / Paris / Sydney / Copenhagen / Berlin / Madrid / Hong Kong / Tokyo

Published by
Wise Publications
14-15 Berners Street, London W1T 3LJ, UK.

Exclusive Distributors:
Music Sales Limited
Distribution Centre, Newmarket Road,
Bury St Edmunds, Suffolk IP33 3YB, UK.
Music Sales Corporation
180 Madison Avenue, 24th Floor, New York NY 10016, USA.
Music Sales Pty Limited
4th floor, Lisgar House, 30-32 Carrington Street,
Sydney, NSW 2000, Australia.

Order No. AM1011406
ISBN 978-1-78558-233-2

Edited by Adrian Hopkins.
Cover designed by Michael Bell Design.
Cover photograph by Michael Ochs Archives / Getty Images.
Printed in the EU.

ALL ALONG THE WATCHTOWER

Words & Music by Bob Dylan

C♯m B A

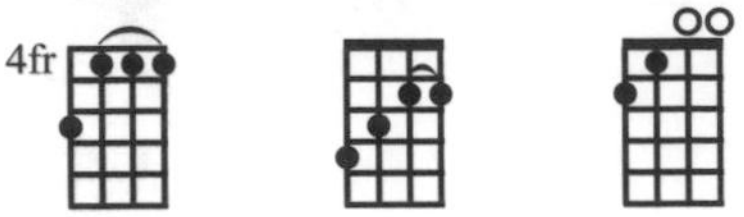

Intro ‖: C♯m B | A B | C♯m B | A B :‖

Verse 1

```
C#m                 B          A              B
   "There must be some way out of here,"
C#m          B             A        B
   Said the joker to the thief
C#m               B            A        B
   "There's too much confusion,
C#m             B      A        B
   I can't get no relief
C#m             B        A                  B
   Businessmen, they drink my wine,
C#m              B         A        B
   Plowmen   dig my earth
C#m           B        A               B
   None of them along the line
C#m               B           A          B
   Know what any of it is worth"
```

Link 1 ‖: C♯m B | A B | C♯m B | A B :‖

Verse 2

```
C#m                B          A       B
   "No reason to get excited,"
C#m                    B      A       B
   The thief, he kindly spoke
C#m                B                 A       B
   "There are many here among us
C#m                     B            A       B
   Who feel that life is but a joke
```

```
         C♯m              B        A                  B
*cont.*     But you and I, we've been through that,
         C♯m            B       A     B
            And this is not our fate
         C♯m          B          A             B
            So let us not talk falsely now,
         C♯m           B          A     B
            The hour is getting late"
```

Link 2 𝄆 C♯m B | A B | C♯m B | A B 𝄇

```
          C♯m     B        A                B
*Verse 3*    All along the watchtower,
          C♯m       B           A    B
             Princes kept the view
          C♯m             B        A                 B
             While all the women came and went,
          C♯m           B        A     B
             Barefoot servants, too
          C♯m         B         A        B
             Outside in the distance
          C♯m         B       A        B
             A wildcat did growl
          C♯m             B               A       B
             Two riders   were approaching,
          C♯m              B      A     B
             The wind began to howl
```

Coda | C♯m B | A B | C♯m B | A B |

| C♯m B | A B | C♯m ‖

ALL I REALLY WANT TO DO

Words & Music by Bob Dylan

A D/E E7 D E9

Intro | A | A ||

Verse 1

D/E A E7 A
I ain't lookin' to compete with you
D A E7 A
Beat or cheat or mistreat you
D/E A E7 A
Simplify you, classify you
D A E7 A
Deny, defy or crucify you
A E9 A D A
All I really want to do____
E7 A D
Is, baby, be friends with you

Link 1 | A D | A D | A E7 |
| A D | A | A ||

Verse 2

A D/E A E7 A
No, and I ain't lookin' to fight with you
D A E7 A
Frighten you or tighten you
D A E7 A
Drag you down or drain you down
D A E7 A
Chain you down or bring you down
A E9 A D A
All I really want to do____
E9 E7 (A)
Is, baby, be friends with you

Link 2 | A D | A D | A E7 | A D E7 | A D | A ||

Verse 3

D/E A E7 A
I ain't lookin' to block you up
D A E7 A
Shock or knock or lock you up
D/E A E7 A
Analyze you, categorize you
D A E7 A
Finalize you or advertise you
A E9 A D A
All I really want to do_____
E9 A D
Is, baby, be friends with you

Link 3 | A E7 | A D | A E7 | A D | A ||

Verse 4

D/E A E7 A
I don't want to straight-face you
D A E7 A
Race or chase you, track or trace you
D A E7 A
Or disgrace you or displace you
D A E7 A
Or define you or confine you
A E9 A D A
All I really want to do_____
E7 A D
Is, baby, be friends with you

Link 4 | A E7 | A D | A E7 | A D | A ||

Verse 5

```
  D/E  A       E7        A
I don't want to meet your kin
D          A       E7     A
Make you spin or do you in
D/E   A        E7    A
Or select you or dissect you
D        A         E7  A
   Or inspect you or reject you
A    E9                A     D    A
All I really want to do____
   E7       A            D
Is, baby, be friends with you
```

Link 5

```
|: A   E7 | A   D   | A   E7 | A   D   :|
|  A   E9 | A   D   | A   E7 | A   D   | A  ||
```

Verse 6

```
D/E     A        E7       A
I don't want to fake you out
D        A          E7        A
Take or shake or forsake you out
D/E   A                    E7      A
I ain't lookin' for you to feel like me
D         A     E7     A
See like me or be like me
A    E9                A     D    A
All I really want to do____
   E7       A            D
Is, baby, be friends with you
```

Outro

```
|: A   E7 | A   D   | A   E7 | A   D   :|
```

Repeat to fade

BALLAD OF A THIN MAN

Words & Music by Bob Dylan

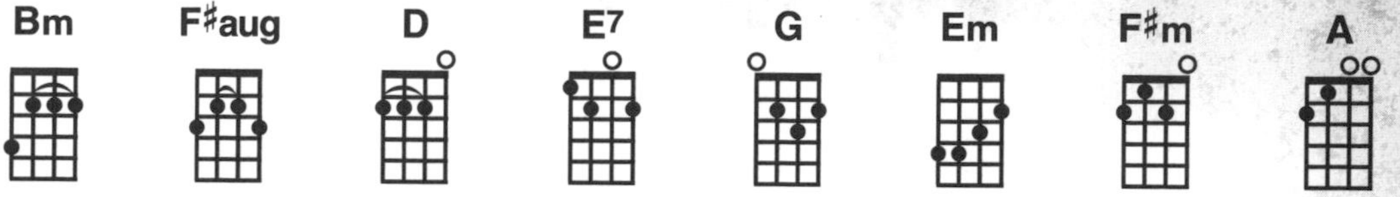

Intro | Bm | Bm | Bm | Bm ||

Verse 1

Bm F♯aug
You walk into the room with your pencil in your hand
D E7
You see somebody naked and you say, "Who is that man?"
G Em
You try so hard but you don't understand
D F♯m Bm
Just what you'll say when you get home

Chorus 1

D F♯m
Be - cause something is happening here
Bm G Bm
But you don't know what it is do you, Mister Jones?

Verse 2

Bm F♯aug
You raise up your head and you ask, "Is this where it is?"
D E7
And somebody points to you and says "It's his"
G
And you say, "What's mine?"
Em
And somebody else says, "Where what is?"
D F♯m Bm
And you say, "Oh my God am I here all a - lone?"

Chorus 2

D F♯m
Because something is happening here
Bm G Bm
But you don't know what it is do you, Mister Jones?

Verse 3

```
Bm                              F#aug
  You hand in your ticket  and you go watch the geek
D                                   E7
  Who immediately walks up to you  when he hears you speak
G                           Em
  And says, "How does it feel to  be such a freak?"
                   D            F#m        Bm
And you say, "Im - possible" as he hands you a bone
```

Chorus 3

```
         D            F#m
Because something is happening here
            Bm                   G            Bm
But you don't know what it is  do you, Mister Jones?
```

Bridge

```
Bm                      D
  You have many contacts  among the lumberjacks
   G                                                  Bm
To  get you facts when someone attacks your imagi - nation
                                D
But nobody has any respect  anyway they already expect you
G                          Em                            A
  To just give a check to tax-deductible charity organi - zations
```

Verse 4

```
Bm                                    F#aug
You've been with the professors and they've all liked your looks
D                                    E7
  With great lawyers you have dis - cussed lepers and crooks
G                                          Em
  You've been through all of F. Scott Fitz - gerald's books
D                  F#m         Bm
  You're very well read it's well known
```

Chorus 4

```
         D            F#m
Because something is happening here
            Bm                  G            Bm
But you don't know what it is do you, Mister Jones?
```

Verse 5

```
Bm                                                F#aug
Well, the sword swallower, he comes up to you and then he kneels
D                                  E7
  He crosses himself and then he clicks his high heels
          G                                   Em
And without further notice he asks you how it feels
                   D              F#m
And he says, "Here is your throat back
                 Bm
Thanks for the loan"
```

```
             D                  F♯m
Chorus 5     Because some - thing is happening here
                       Bm                    G              Bm
             But you don't know what it is   do you, Mister Jones?

             Bm                                   F♯aug
Verse 6      Now you see this one-eyed midget    shouting the word "NOW"
             D                                 E7
               And you say, "For what reason?"    And he says, "How?"
             G
               And you say, "What does this mean?"
                      Em
             And he screams back, "You're a cow
             D                F♯m          Bm
             Give me some milk or else go home"

             D                          F♯m
Chorus 6     Because something is happening here
                       Bm                    G              Bm
             But you don't know what it is   do you, Mister Jones?

             Bm                                       F♯aug
Verse 7      Well, you walk into the room like a camel and then you frown
             D                                                E7
               You put your eyes in your pocket and your    nose on the ground
             G                                Em
               There ought to be a law a - gainst you comin' around
                 D                     F♯m       Bm
             You should be made to wear ear - phones

             D                            F♯m
Chorus 7       Because something is happening here
                       Bm                    G              Bm
             But you don't know what it is   do you, Mister Jones?

Outro        ||: Bm    | Bm    | Bm    | Bm    :||   Repeat to fade
```

BEYOND HERE LIES NOTHIN'

Music by Bob Dylan
Words by Bob Dylan & Robert Hunter

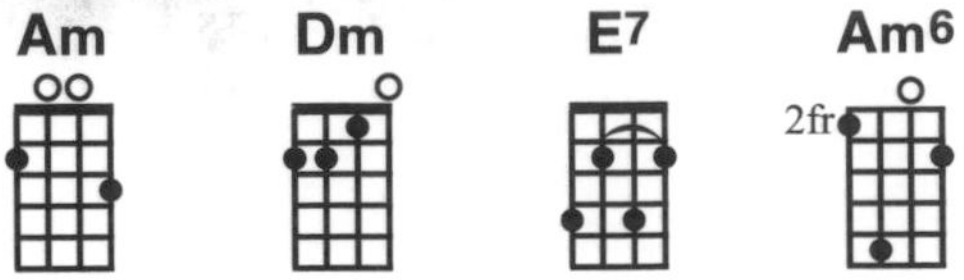

Intro | Am | Am | Am | Am |
| Dm | Dm | Am | Am |
| E7 | Dm | Am ||

Verse 1
N.C. Am
I love you pretty baby

You're the only love I've ever known
Dm
Just as long as you stay with me
Am
The whole world is my throne
E7 Dm
Beyond here lies no - thin'
Am
Nothin' we can call our own

Verse 2
N.C. Am
I'm movin' after midnight

Down boulevards of broken cars
Dm
Don't know what to do with - out it
Am
Without this love that we call ours
E7 Dm
Beyond here lies no - thin'
Am
Nothin' but the moon and stars

Instrumental 1 | Am | Am | Am | Am |
| Dm | Dm | Am | Am |
| E7 | Dm | Am ||

Verse 3

N.C. Am
Down every street there's a window

And every window made of glass

Dm
We'll keep on lovin' pretty baby

Am
For as long as love will last

E7
Beyond here lies no - thin'

Dm Am
But the mountains of the past

Instrumental 2 ||: Am | Am | Am | Am |
| Dm | Dm | Am | Am |
| E7 | Dm | Am | Am :||

Verse 4

N.C. Am
My ship is in the harbor

And the sails are spread

Dm
Listen to me pretty baby

Am
Lay your hand upon my head

E7 Dm
Beyond here lies no - thin'

Am
Nothin' done and nothin' said

Outro | Am | Am | Am | Am |
| Dm | Dm | Am | Am |
| E7 | Dm | Am | N.C. | Am6 ||

BLIND WILLIE McTELL

Words & Music by Bob Dylan

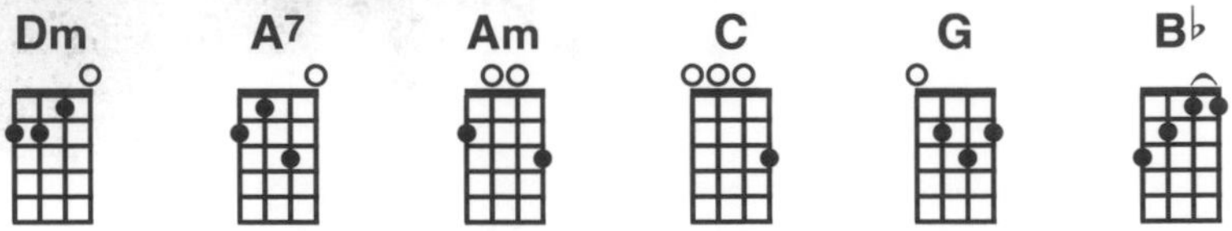

To match original recording, tune ukulele up one semitone

Intro | Dm | Dm A7 | Dm | Dm ||

Verse 1

Dm A7 Dm Am Dm
Seen the arrow on_ the doorpost

A7 Dm Am Dm
Saying, "This land is condemned

A7 C G
All the way from New Orleans__

B♭ C Dm Am Dm
To Jerusalem"

A7 Dm Am Dm
I traveled_ through East Texas

A7 Dm Am Dm
Where many martyrs fell__

A7 C G
And I know no one can sing the blues

B♭ C Dm Am Dm
Like Blind Willie_ McTell

Verse 2

Dm A7 Dm Am Dm
Well, I heard that hoot owl singing

A7 Dm Am Dm
As they were taking down the tents

A7 C G
The stars above the barren trees__

B♭ C Dm Am Dm
Were his only audience

A7 Dm Am Dm
Them charcoal gypsy maidens

A7 Dm Am Dm
Can strut their feathers well___

cont.

A7 C G
But nobody can sing the blues__
B♭ C Dm Am Dm
Like Blind Willie_ McTell

Verse 3

Dm A7 Dm Am Dm
See them big plantations burning
A7 Dm Am Dm
Hear the cracking of the whips
A7 C G
Smell that sweet magnolia blooming
B♭ C Dm
See the ghosts of_ slavery ships
A7 Dm Am Dm
I can hear them tribes a-moaning
A7 Dm
Hear the undertaker's bell
A7 C G
Nobody can sing the blues__
B♭ C Dm Am Dm
Like Blind_ Willie McTell

Verse 4

Dm A7 Dm Am Dm
There's a woman_ by the river__
A7 Dm Am Dm
With some fine young handsome man
A7 C G
He's dressed up like a squire
B♭ C Dm
Bootlegged whiskey in his hand__
A7 Dm Am Dm
There's a chain gang on the highway
A7 Dm Am Dm
I can hear them rebels yell
A7 C G
And I know no one can sing the blues
B♭ C Dm Am Dm
Like Blind Willie McTell

Link

| Dm A7 | Dm Am Dm | Dm A7 | Dm Am Dm |

| Dm A7 | C G | B♭ C | Dm Am Dm | Dm Am Dm ||

Verse 5

```
         Dm      A7                   Dm   Am   Dm
Well, God is in His heaven
              A7                 Dm   Am   Dm
And we all_ want what's His
                   A7                C              G
But power and greed and corruptible seed__
B♭            C              Dm
Seem to be all that there is
              A7                      Dm   Am   Dm
I'm gazing out the window
             A7               Dm   Am   Dm
Of the St. James Hotel__
                  A7    C                G
And I know no   one   can sing the blues
B♭                 C           Dm   Am   Dm
   Like Blind Willie McTell
```

Coda

```
| Dm   A7  | Dm  Am  Dm | Dm   A7  | Dm  Am  Dm |
| Dm   A7  | C    G     | B♭   C   | Dm  Am  Dm |
| Dm   A7  | Dm  Am  Dm | Dm   A7  | Dm  Am  Dm |
| Dm   A7  | C    G     | B♭   C   | Dm         ||
```

BROWNSVILLE GIRL

Words & Music by Bob Dylan & Sam Sheppard

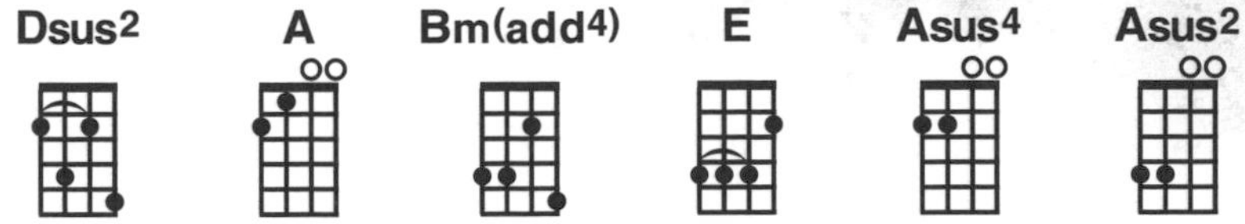

Intro ||: Dsus2 A Bm(add4) E | A Asus4 A :||

Verse 1

A Dsus2
Well, there was this movie I seen one time
Bm(add4)
About a man riding 'cross the desert
E A Asus4 A
And it starred Gregory Peck

He was shot down by a hungry kid
Dsus2
Trying to make a name for him - self
Bm(add4)
The townspeople wanted to crush that kid down
E A
And string him up by the neck

Verse 2

A Dsus2
Well, the marshal, now he beat that kid to a bloody pulp
Bm(add4) E
As the dying gunfighter lay in the sun
A Asus4 A
And gasped for his last breath

"Turn him loose, let him go,
Dsus2
Let him say he outdrew me fair and square
Bm(add4)
I want him to feel what it's like
E A Asus4 A
To every moment face his death"

Verse 3

```
A                                                 Dsus2
Well, I keep seeing this stuff and it just comes a-rolling in
                Bm(add4)
And you know it blows right through me
      E              A  Asus4  A
Like a ball and chain

You know I can't believe we've lived so long
                          Dsus2
And are still so far apart
   Bm(add4)                    E                  A       Asus4  A
The memory of you keeps callin' after me like a roll - in' train
```

Verse 4

```
A                                                         Dsus2
I can still see the day that you came to me on the painted desert
          Bm(add4)                 E              A
In your busted down Ford and your platform heels

I could never figure out why you chose
                              Dsus2
That particular place to meet
                Bm(add4)
Ah, but you were right.
                E               A        Asus4  A
It was perfect as I got in behind the wheel
```

Verse 5

```
A                                          Dsus2
Well, we drove that car all night into San An - ton'
          Bm(add4)                   E                 A
And we slept near the Alamo, your skin was so tender and soft

Way down in Mexico you went out to find a doctor
        Dsus2
And you never came back
            Bm(add4)
I would have gone on after you
          E                          A
But I didn't feel like letting my head get blown off
```

Verse 6

```
A
Well, we're drivin' this car
                                                 Dsus2
And the sun is comin' up over the Rock - ies
                  Bm(add4)
Now I know she ain't you but she's here
       E                                       A     Asus4  A
And she's got that dark rhythm in her soul

But I'm too over the edge and I ain't in the mood anymore
                        Dsus2
To remember the times when I was your only man
                     Bm(add4)
And she don't want to remind me.
                   E                            A     Asus4  A
She knows this car would go out of con - trol
```

Chorus 1

```
A                           Dsus2
Brownsville girl with your Brownsville curls
Bm(add4)        E                          A     Asus4  A
Teeth like pearls shining like the moon a - bove
                       Dsus2
Brownsville girl, show me all around the world
Bm(add4)        E                A
Brownsville girl, you're my honey love
```

Verse 7

```
A
Well, we crossed the panhandle
                                         Dsus2
And then we headed towards Ama - rillo
                                         Bm(add4)
We pulled up where Henry Porter used to live.
                E                                    A     Asus4
He owned a wreckin' lot outside of town about a mile
A
Ruby was in the backyard hanging clothes,
                                  Dsus2
She had her red hair tied back.

She saw us come rolling up in a trail of dust
Bm(add4)                                    E
  She said, "Henry ain't here but you can come on in,
                     A                Asus4  A
He'll be back in a little while"
```

Verse 8

A
Then she told us how times were tough

Dsus2
And about how she was thinkin' of bummin' a ride

Back to from where she started

Bm(add4) E A
But ya know, she changed the subject every time money came up

Asus4 A
She said, "Welcome to the land of the living dead"

Dsus2
You could tell she was so broken hearted

Bm(add4)
She said, "Even the swap meets around here

E A Asus4 A
Are getting pretty corrupt"

Verse 9

A Dsus2
"How far are y'all going?" Ruby asked us with a sigh

Bm(add4) E A
"We're going all the way 'til the wheels fall off and burn

'Til the sun peels the paint

Dsus2
And the seat covers fade and the water moccasin dies"

Bm(add4)
Ruby just smiled and said,

E A Asus2 A
"Ah, you know some babies never learn"

Verse 10

A
Something about that movie though,

Dsus2
Well I just can't get it out of my head

Bm(add4)
But I can't remember why I was in it

E A
Or what part I was supposed to play

Asus2 A
All I re - member about it was Gregory Peck

Dsus2
And the way people moved

Bm(add4) E A
And a lot of them seemed to be lookin' my way

```
Chorus 2    A                               Dsus2
            Brownsville girl with your Brownsville curls
            Bm(add4)          E                      A
            Teeth like pearls shining like the moon a - bove
            A                                  Dsus2
            Brownsville girl, show me all around the world
            Bm(add4)          E                A
            Brownsville girl, you're my honey love

Sax. solo 1 | A           | Dsus2        | Bm(add4)  E | A          ||

            A                                             Dsus2
Verse 11    Well, they were looking for somebody with a pompadour
                 Bm(add4)          E                   A
            I was crossin' the street    when shots rang out
                                                      Dsus2
            I didn't know whether to duck or to run, so I ran
                          Bm(add4)                      E                    A
            "We got him cornered in the churchyard," I heard somebody shout

            A
Verse 12    Well, you saw my picture in the Corpus Christi Tribune.
                                                  Dsus2
            Underneath it, it said, "A man with no alibi"
                                Bm(add4)                  E               A
            You went out on a limb to testify for me,    you said I was with you

            Then when I saw you break down in front of the judge
                   Dsus2
            And cry real tears
                        Bm(add4)           E        A
            It was the best acting I saw anybody do

            A
Verse 13    Now I've always been the kind of person that doesn't like to trespass
                                        Dsus2
            But sometimes you just find yourself over the line
                                 Bm(add4)                  E                 A
            Oh if there's an o - riginal thought out there,    I could use it right now

            You know, I feel pretty good, but that ain't sayin' much.
                                        Dsus2
            I could feel a whole lot better
            Bm(add4)                             E              A
              If you were just here by my side to show me how
```

Verse 14

A
Well, I'm standin' in line in the rain

Dsus2
To see a movie starring Gregory Peck

Bm(add4) E A
Yeah, but you know it's not the one that I had in mind

Dsus2
He's got a new one out now, I don't even know what it's about

Bm(add4) E A
But I'll see him in anything so I'll stand in line

Chorus 3

A Dsus2
Brownsville girl with your Brownsville curls

Bm(add4) E A Asus4 A
Teeth like pearls shining like the moon a - bove

Dsus2
Brownsville girl, show me all around the world

Bm(add4) E A
Brownsville girl, you're my honey love

Sax. solo 2

𝄆 A | Dsus2 | Bm(add4) E | A 𝄇

Verse 15

A
You know, it's funny how things never turn out

Dsus2
The way you had 'em planned

Bm(add4)
The only thing we knew for sure about Henry Porter

E A
Is that his name wasn't Henry Porter

And you know there was somethin' about you baby that I liked

Dsus2
That was always too good for this world

Bm(add4) E
Just like you always said there was somethin' about me you liked

A
That I left behind in the French Quarter

```
            A
Verse 16    Strange how people who suffer together have stronger connections
                                   Dsus2
            Than people who are most content
                                  Bm(add4)
            I don't have any re - grets,
                                  E                          A
            They can talk about me plenty when I'm gone

            You always said people don't do what they believe in,
                                 Dsus2
            They just do what's most convenient, then they repent
                 Bm(add4)
            And I always said, "Hang on to me, baby,
                 E                            A
            And let's hope that the roof stays on"

            A                                     Dsus2
Verse 17    There was a movie I seen one time, I think I sat through it twice
              Bm(add4)                          E                  A
            I don't remember who I was or where I was bound
                                                          Dsus2
            All I remember about it was it starred Gregory Peck,

            He wore a gun and he was shot in the back
            Bm(add4)                            E                           A
            Seems like a long time ago, long before the stars were torn down

              A                               Dsus2
Chorus 4    ||: Brownsville girl with your Brownsville curls
            Bm(add4)           E                          A      Asus4   A
            Teeth like pearls shining like the moon a - bove
                              Dsus2
            Brownsville girl, show me all around the world
            Bm(add4)           E                    A
            Brownsville girl, you're my honey love :||  Play 3 times to fade
```

BLOWIN' IN THE WIND

Words & Music by Bob Dylan

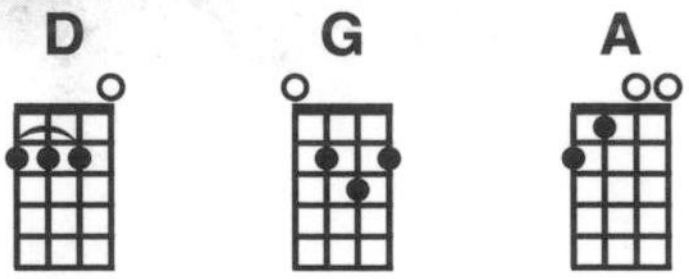

Intro | D ||

Verse 1

D G A D
How many roads must a man walk down
G D
Before you call him a man?
G A D
Yes, 'n' how many seas must a white dove sail
G A
Before she sleeps in the sand?
D G A D
Yes, 'n' how many times must the cannonballs fly
G D
Before they're forever banned?

Chorus 1

G A D G
The answer, my friend, is blowin' in the wind
A D
The answer is blowin' in the wind

Link 1 | G A | D G | G A | D ||

Verse 2

```
D            G            A              D
How many years can a mountain exist
                 G              D
Before it's washed to the sea?
                              G             A            D
Yes, 'n' how many years can some people exist
                           G             A
Before they're allowed to be free?
             D             G            A            D
Yes, 'n' how many times can a man turn his head
                       G            D
Pretending he just doesn't see?
```

Chorus 2 As Chorus 1

Link 2 | G A | D G | G A | D ||

Verse 3

```
D           G               A        D
How many times must a man look up
                       G     D
Before he can see the sky?
                              G         A        D
Yes, 'n' how many ears must one man have
                       G            A
Before he can hear people cry?
             D            G                A          D
Yes, 'n' how many deaths will it take till he knows
                        G                    D
That too many people have died?
```

Chorus 3 As Chorus 1

Coda | G A | D G | G A | D ||

CHANGING OF THE GUARDS

Words & Music by Bob Dylan

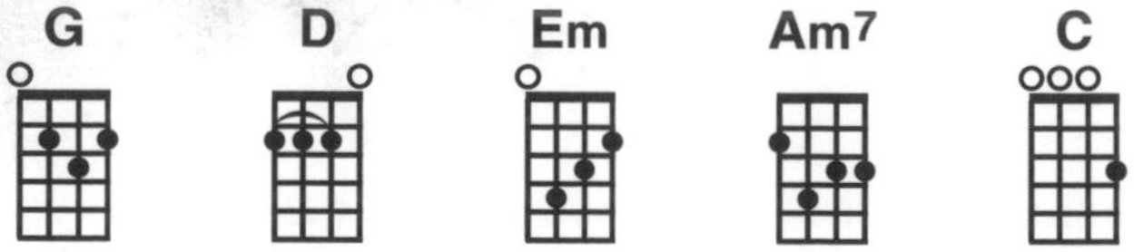

To match original recording, tune ukulele up one semitone

Intro | G *(fade in)* ||

Verse 1

G D Em
Six - teen years
Am7 G D Em
Sixteen banners united over the field
C D
Where the good shepherd grieves
Em Am7 G D
Desperate men, desperate women divided
Em C D G
Spreading their wings 'neath the fall-ing leaves

Verse 2

G D Em
Fortune calls
Am7 G D Em
I stepped forth from the shadows, to the marketplace
C D Em
Merchants and thieves, hungry for power, my last deal gone down
Am7 G D Em
She's smelling sweet like the meadows where she was born
C D G
On midsummer's eve, near the tower

Link 1

| G D | C | G D | C |

| G D | C D | G C ||

Verse 3

G   D   Em
  The cold-blooded moon
     Am7   G   D
The captain waits above the celebration
               Em   C   D
Sending his thoughts to a   beloved maid
                  Em   Am7 G   D
Whose ebony face is be-yond communication
                 Em   C   D   G
The captain is down but still believing that his love will be repaid

Verse 4

      G   D   Em
They shaved her head
         Am7   G   D
She was torn between   Jupiter and Apollo
                    Em   C   D
A messenger arrived with a black nightingale
                   Em   Am7 G   D
I seen her on the stairs and I   couldn't help but follow
             Em   C   D   G
Follow her down past the fountain where they lift - ed her veil

Link 2

| G D | C | G D | C |

| G D | C D | G C ||

Verse 5

G   D   Em
  I stumbled to my feet
  Am7   G   D
I rode past destruction in the ditches
          Em   C   D
With the stitches still mending 'neath a heart-shaped tattoo
            Em   Am7 G   D
Renegade priests and   treacherous young witches
        Em   C   D   G
Were handing out the flowers that I'd   given to you

Verse 6

```
    G      D   Em
The palace of  mirrors
Am7        G               D
Where dog  soldiers are reflected
              Em            C          D
The endless road and the wailing of chimes
             Em      Am7       G              D
The empty rooms where her memory is protected
            Em                            C         D        G
Where the angels' voices whisper to the souls of previous times
```

Link 3

```
| G    D  | C         | G    D  | C         |
| G    D  | C    D    | G    C  ||
```

Verse 7

```
    G     D   Em
She wakes him up
     Am7        G                D
Forty-eight hours later, the sun is breaking
              Em                C                  D
Near broken chains, mountain laurel and rolling rocks
                   Em      Am7 G                         D
She's begging to know what measures he now will be taking
                  Em                                 C      D        G
He's pulling her down and she's clutching on to his  long golden locks
```

Verse 8

```
G      D        Em
Gentlemen, he said
Am7   G                  D                        Em
I don't need your organization, I've shined your shoes
                   C                           D
I've moved your mountains and marked your cards
             Em             Am7          G        D
But Eden is burning, either brace yourself  for elimination
              Em                                   C        D      G
Or else your hearts must have the courage for the changing of the guards
```

Link 4

```
| G    D  | C       | G    D  | C       |
| G    D  | C    D  | G    C  ||
```

Verse 9

```
G       D   Em
Peace will come
Am7        G          D                              Em
With tranquillity and splendor on the wheels of fire
           C               D                             Em
But will bring us no reward when her false idols fall
Am7 G                    D                 Em
And   cruel death surrenders with its pale ghost retreating
                C               D              G
Between the King and the Queen of Swords
```

Coda

```
| Em      | Em  Am7 | G       | D       |
| Em      | Em      | C       | D       |
| Em      | Em  Am7 | G       | D       |
| Em      | Em      | C    D  | G       |
| G    D  | C       | G    D  | C       |
| G    D  | C    D  | G       ||  To fade
```

CHIMES OF FREEDOM

Words & Music by Bob Dylan

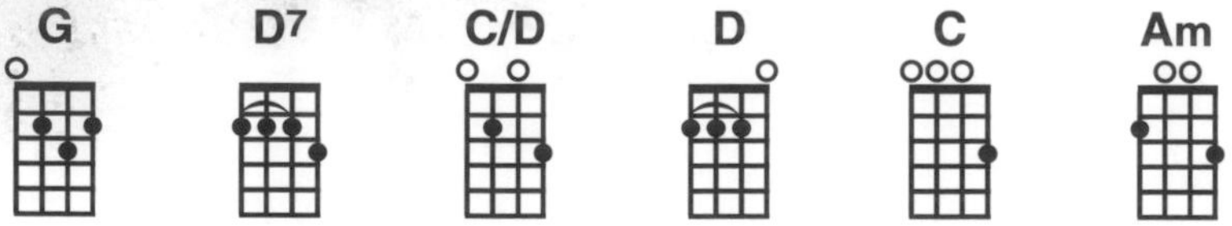

Intro | G ||

Verse 1

G D7 G C/D G
Far between sundown's finish an' midnight's broken toll
C/D G D G C G
We ducked inside the doorway, thunder crashing
C/D G C/D G C/D
As majestic bells of bolts struck shadows in the sounds
G C/D G D G C G
Seeming to be the chimes of freedom flashing
D G C G
Flashing for the warriors whose strength is not to fight
C G Am D7
Flashing for the refugees on the unarmed road of flight
G D7 G C
An' for each an' ev'ry underdog soldier in the night
G D7 G C G
An' we gazed upon the chimes of freedom flashing

Verse 2

G C/D G C/D G C/D
In the city's melted furnace, unexpectedly we watched
G C/D D G C G
With faces hidden while the walls were tightening
C/D G C/D G C/D
As the echo of the wedding bells before the blowin' rain
G C/D D G C G
Dissolved into the bells of the lightning

```
             D                  G
cont.        Tolling for the rebel, tolling for the rake
             C                          G     Am            D7
             Tolling for the luckless,   the abandoned an' forsaked
             G                C         G          C
             Tolling for the outcast, burnin' constantly at stake
                   G             C      G     D7    G        C  G
             An' we gazed upon the chimes of   freedom flashing

                        G          C/D            G    C/D   G    C/D
Verse 3      Through the mad mystic hammering of the wild ripping hail
                G   C/D     D               G   C  G
             The sky  cracked its poems in naked wonder
                                         C/D      G    C/D  G     C/D
             That the clinging of the church bells blew far into the breeze
                   G   C/D   D               G      C  G
             Leaving only bells of lightning and its thunder
             D                    G
               Striking for the gentle, striking for the kind
             C                  G            Am           D
             Striking for the guardians and protectors of the mind
                   G            D7   G                      C
             An' the unpawned painter behind beyond his rightful time
                   G             C        D7      G       C  G
             An' we gazed upon the chimes of freedom flashing

                        G            C/D       G     C/D     G   C/D
Verse 4      Through the wild cathedral evening the rain unraveled tales
                   G       C/D     D              G    C  G  D7
             For the disrobed faceless forms of no position
             G           C/D            G       C/D        G      C/D
             Tolling for the tongues with no place to bring their thoughts
                 G      C/D       D          G   C  G
             All down in taken-for-granted situations
             D                         G
             Tolling for the deaf an' blind, tolling for the mute
                         C                    G          Am         D
             Tolling for the mistreated, mateless mother, the mistitled prostitute
                   G              D7          G                 C
             For the misdemeanor outlaw, chased an' cheated by pursuit
                   G             C        D7      G       C
             An' we gazed upon the chimes of freedom flashing

Link 1       | D    | G    | G    | G    | G    ||
```

Verse 5

```
     G                          C/D          G        C/D     G        C/D
Even though a cloud's white curtain in a far-off corner flashed
        G           C/D         D                         G     C  G
An' the hypnotic splattered mist was slowly lifting
                                C/D       G          C/D       G     C/D
Electric light still struck like arrows, fired but for the ones
   G            C/D      D                      G        C  G
Condemned to drift or else be kept from drifting
D                                        G
Tolling for the searching ones, on their   speechless, seeking trail
        C                         G            Am                D7
For the lonesome-hearted lovers with too personal a tale
    G                      D                 G                 C
An' for each unharmful, gentle soul misplaced inside a jail
        G                 C          D7          G        C  G  D7
An' we gazed upon the chimes of freedom flashing
```

Link 2

G	C/D	G	C/D G C	G
C D7	C C	G	G	G ‖

Verse 6

```
G                 C/D            G           C/D             G      C/D
Starry-eyed an' laughing as I recall when we were caught
G                C/D     D                              G      C  G
Trapped by no track of hours for they hanged suspended
                            C/D         G            C/D       G       C/D
As we listened one last time an' we watched with one last look
G             C/D  D                          G        C  G
Spellbound an'   swallowed 'til the tolling ended
D                                   G
Tolling for the aching ones whose wounds cannot be nursed
        C                         G                Am                     D7
For the countless confused, accused, misused, strung-out ones an' worse
         G                   D7              G             C
An' for every hung-up person in the whole wide universe
         G                C       G      D7        G       C  D7  G
An' we gazed upon the chimes of   freedom flashing
```

DARK EYES

Words & Music by Bob Dylan

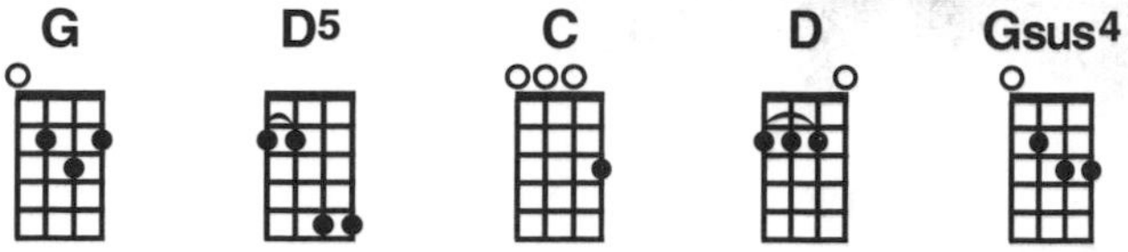

Intro

```
||: G          D5    G   | C          D        |
 |  G          D5    G   | C          G       :||
```

Verse 1

```
           G        D5  G      C     D
Oh, the gentle - men are talk - ing
           G          D5         G           C    G
And the midnight moon is on the riverside
                         D5  G       C       D
They're drinking up  and walk - ing
       G    D5   G  C      G
And it is time for me to slide
Gsus4 G             C      D
I        live in an - other world
         Gsus4 G                    C         D
Where life      and  death are memorized
               G          D5       G      C         D
Where the earth is strung with lovers' pearls
       G    D5  G  C      G
And all I see are dark eyes
```

Harmonica 1

```
|  G          D5    G   | C          D        |
|  G          D5    G   | C          G       ||
```

```
             G        D5   G   C      D
Verse 2      A cock is crowing far away
                      G      D5   G       C      G
             And an - other sol - dier's deep in prayer
                             D5    G  C          D
             Some mother's child has gone a - stray,
             G           D5  G    C     G
             She can't find him any - where
                Gsus4  G                C     D
             But I          can hear  an - other drum
             Gsus4 G             C          D
             Beat - ing for the dead that rise
                     G         D5    G     C       D
             Whom nature's beast fears as they come
                  G   D5 G   C    G
             And all I see are dark eyes

Harmonica 2  | G          D5     G   | C        D        |

             | G          D5     G   | C        G        ||
```

```
             G          D5  G C        D
Verse 3      They tell me to be dis - creet
                  G       D5     G  C        G
             For all in - tend - ed purpos - es
                          D5  G   C        D
             They tell me re - venge is sweet
                            G           D5     G   C      G
             And from where they stand, I'm sure it is
                 Gsus4   G          C        D
             But I     feel nothing for their game
                      Gsus4 G             C       D
             Where beau - ty goes un - recog - nized
             G    D5  G  C          D
             All I feel is  heat and flame
                   G   D5 G  C    G
             And all I see are dark eyes

Harmonica 3  |: G         D5     G   | C        D        |

             | G          D5     G   | C        G       :|
```

Verse 4

```
              G              D5     G  C          D
Oh, the French girl, she's in par - a - dise
            G           D5   G  C       G
And a drunken man is at the wheel
              D5    G  C          D
Hunger pays a  heavy price
            G       D5     G     C           G
To the falling gods of speed and steel
      Gsus4  G                      C         D
Oh, time    is short and the days are sweet
       Gsus4   G                     C            D
And pas    -   sion rules the arrow that flies
    G        D5    G  C       D
A million fac - es at my feet
      G    D5  G  C    G
But all I see are dark eyes
```

Outro

```
|: G        D5       G | C          D  |
 | G        D5       G | C          G :|
 | Gsus4  G            | C          D  |
 | Gsus4  G            | C          D  |
 | G        D5       G | C          D  |
 | G        D5       G | C          G  |
 | G        D5       G | G     C    G(fermata) ||
```

DESOLATION ROW

Words & Music by Bob Dylan

E
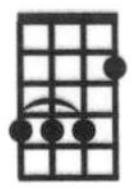
E(add4)
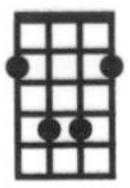
A
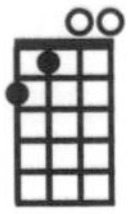
B
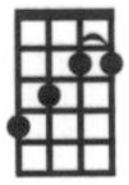

Intro | E E(add4) | E E(add4) | E E(add4) ||

Verse 1

```
E                E(add4) E           E(add4) E
   They're selling  postcards of the    hanging
           A                     E
They're painting the passports brown
      B
The beauty parlor is filled with sailors
A                    E
   The circus is in town
                        E(add4)   E
Here comes the blind commissioner
          A          E
They've got him in a trance
      B
One hand is tied to the tight-rope walker
A                       E
   The other is in his pants
          A
And the riot squad they're restless
       E                   A
They need somewhere to go
   E                    B
As Lady and I look out tonight
       A           E       E(add4)  E   E(add4)
From   Desolation Row
```

Verse 2

```
E          E(add4)       E
Cinderella, she seems so easy
   A                           E
"It takes one to know one," she smiles
     B
And puts her hands in her back pockets
A              E     E(add4)   E
  Bette Davis style
              E(add4)      E
And in comes Romeo, he's moaning
          A                 E
"You Be - long to Me I Be - lieve"
     B
And someone says, "You're in the wrong place my friend
A            E
  You better leave"
        A
And the only sound that's left
E                    A
After the ambulances go
  E          B
Is Cinderella sweeping up
   A           E     E(add4)  E  E(add4)
On Desolation Row
```

Verse 3

```
E E(add4) E       E(add4) E
  Now the moon is almost  hidden
    A                     E
The stars are beginning to hide
    B
The fortune-telling lady
    A                         E    E(add4)  E
Has even taken all her things inside
                E(add4)    E
All except for Cain and A - bel
        A                   E
And the hunchback of Notre Dame
B
Everybody is making love
   A              E
Or else expecting rain
        A
And the Good Samaritan, he's dressing
            E            A
He's getting ready for the show
     E           B
He's going to the carnival tonight
   A             E     E(add4)  E  E(add4)
On   Desolation Row
```

Verse 4

```
E                              E(add4)   E
Now Ophelia, she's 'neath the window
    A                E
For her I feel so a - fraid
       B
On her twenty-second birthday
          A               E
She al - ready is an old maid
                    E(add4)   E
To her, death is quite ro - mantic
    A               E
She wears an iron vest
            B
Her pro - fession's her religion
    A                   E
Her sin is her lifeless - ness
     A
And though her eyes are fixed upon
E                A
Noah's great rain - bow
  E                 B
She spends her time peeking
     A             E       E(add4)  E  E(add4)
Into    Desolation Row
```

Verse 5

```
E E(add4) E             E(add4)   E
          Einstein, dis - guised as Robin Hood
          A               E
With his memories in a trunk
B
Passed this way an hour ago
          A                E
With his friend, a jealous monk
                   E(add4)     E
He looked so im - maculately frightful
     A                E
As he bummed a ciga - rette
          B
Then he went off sniffing drainpipes
    A                  E
And reciting the alpha - bet
           A
Now you would not think to look at him
             E             A
But he was famous long a - go
    E                  B
For playing the electric violin
   A             E       E(add4)  E  E(add4)
On Desolation Row
```

Verse 6

```
E     E(add4)  E            E(add4)   E
   Dr.          Filth, he keeps his world
      A                   E
In - side of a leather cup
     B
But all his sexless patients
          A                     E     E(add4)
They're trying to blow it up
          E                E(add4) E
Now his nurse, some local     loser
          A                          E
She's in charge of the cyanide hole
          B
And she also keeps the cards that read
        A               E
"Have Mercy on His Soul"
A
They all play on pennywhistles
E                     A
You can hear them blow
        E                      B
If you lean your head out far enough
      A            E        E(add4)  E  E(add4)
From   Desolation Row
```

Verse 7

```
E                               E(add4)     E
Across the street they've nailed the curtains
                    A            E
They're getting ready for the feast
    B
The Phantom of the Opera
  A                     E
A perfect image of a priest
                       E(add4)     E
They're spoonfeed - ing Casa - nova
       A                      E
To get him to feel more as - sured
               B
Then they'll kill him with self-confidence
      A                  E
After poisoning him with words
          A
And the Phantom's shouting to skinny girls
     E                            A
"Get Outa Here If You Don't Know
     E                   B
Casanova is just being punished for going
   A           E        E(add4)  E  E(add4)
To   Desolation Row"
```

Verse 8

E E(add4) E E(add4) E
Now at midnight all the agents
A E
And the superhuman crew
B
Come out and round up everyone
A E E(add4)
That knows more than they do
E E(add4) E
Then they bring them to the factory
A E
Where the heart-attack ma - chine
B
Is strapped across their shoulders
A E
And then the kero - sene
A
Is brought down from the castles
E A
By in - surance men who go
E B
Check to see that nobody is e - scaping
A E E(add4) E E(add4)
To Desolation Row

Verse 9

E E(add4) E E(add4) E
Praise be to Nero's Neptune
A E
The Titanic sails at dawn
B
And everybody's shouting
A E E(add4)
"Which Side Are You On?"
E E(add4) E
And Ezra Pound and T. S. Eliot
A E
Fighting in the captain's tower
B
While calypso singers laugh at them
A E
And fishermen hold flowers
A
Be - tween the windows of the sea
E A
Where lovely mermaids flow
E B
And nobody has to think too much
A E E(add4) E E(add4)
About Desolation Row

Instrumental 1 | E E(add4) | E | A | E |
B	B	A	E
E E(add4)	E	A	E
B	B	A	E
A	A	E	A
E	B	A	E E(add4)	

```
                E    E(add4) E                 E(add4) E
Verse 10             Yes, I received your letter     yesterday
                       A                                E
                (A - bout the time the doorknob broke)
                               B
                When you asked how I was doing
                     A                      E
                Was that some kind of joke?
                                  E(add4)  E
                All these people that you mention
                      A                           E
                Yes, I know them, they're quite lame
                         B
                I had to rearrange their faces
                           A                     E
                And give them all another name
                      A
                Right now I can't read too good
                       E                              A
                Don't send me no more letters, no
                E                B
                Not unless you mail them
                      A            E         E(add4)
                From Desolation Row
```

Instrumental 2 | E E(add4) | E | A | E |
B	B	A	E
E E(add4)	E	A	E
B	B	A	E
A	A	E	A
E	B	A	E	

DIGNITY

Words & Music by Bob Dylan

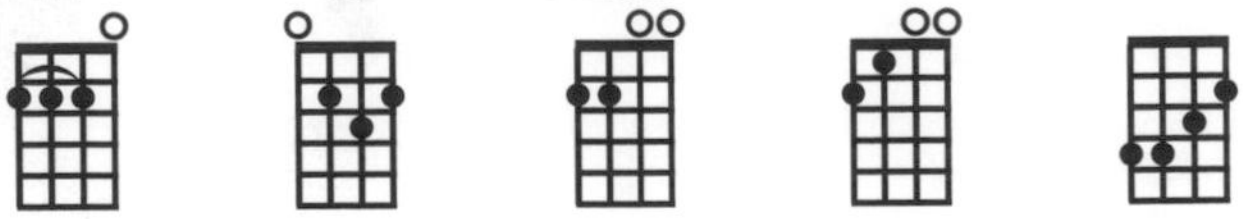

To match original recording, tune ukulele up a semitone

```
Intro      | D        | G  D     | D        | G  D     ||

           D                                  G      D
Verse 1    Fat man lookin' in a blade of steel
                                          G      D
           Thin man lookin' at his last meal
           G                                       D
              Hollow man lookin' in a cotton - field
                         Asus4  D
           For dignity

           D                                     G      D
Verse 2    Wise man lookin' in a blade of grass
                                                        G      D
           Young man lookin' in the shadows that pass
           G                                              D
              Poor man lookin' through painted glass
                         Asus4  D
           For dignity

           A
Bridge 1      Somebody got murdered on New Year's Eve
           G                                       D
              Somebody said dignity was the first to leave
           G                   D
              I went into the city,   went into the town
                          Em                            Asus4  D
           Went into the land of the midnight sun
```

Verse 3

D G D
Searchin' high, searchin' low

Searchin' everywhere I know

G D
Askin' the cops wher - ever I go

Asus4 D
Have you seen dignity?

Link 1

| D | G D ||

Verse 4

D
Blind man breakin' out of a trance

G D
Puts both his hands in the pockets of chance

G D
Hopin' to find one circum - stance

Asus4 D
Of dignity

Verse 5

D G D
I went to the wedding of Mary Lou

G D
She said, "I don't want nobody see me talkin' to you"

G D
Said she could get killed if she told me what she knew

Asus4 D
About dignity

Bridge 2

A
I went down where the vultures feed

G D
I would've gone deeper, but there wasn't any need

G D
Heard the tongues of angels and the tongues of men

Em A
Wasn't any difference to me

Verse 6

D G D
Chilly wind sharp as a razor blade

G D
House on fire, debts un - paid

G D
Gonna stand at the window, gonna ask the maid

Asus4 D
Have you seen dig - nity?

```
Link 2          | D       | G  D    | D       | G  D  ||

                D                                     G     D
Verse 7         Drinkin' man listens to the voice he hears
                                                        G      D
                In a crowded room full of covered-up mirrors
                G                                  D
                   Lookin' into the lost forgotten years
                            Asus4  D
                For dignity

                D                                      G      D
Verse 8         Met Prince Phillip at the home of the blues
                                                       G              D
                Said he'd give me information if his name wasn't used
                             G                  D
                He wanted money up front, said he was abused
                            Asus4  D
                By dignity

                A
Bridge 3           Footprints runnin' 'cross the silver sand
                G                        D
                   Steps goin' down into tattoo land
                         G                          D
                I met the sons of darkness and the sons of light
                      Em                      A
                In the bordertowns of des - pair

                D                      G              D
Verse 9         Got no place to fade, got no coat
                                                 G      D
                I'm on the rollin' river in a jerkin' boat
                G                          D
                   Tryin' to read a note somebody wrote
                               Asus4  D
                About dignity

Instrumental    | D       | G  D    | D       | G       D |

                | G       | D       | D       | Asus4  D  ||
```

```
             D                                  G     D
Verse 10     Sick man lookin' for the doctor's cure

                                           G         D
             Lookin' at his hands for the lines that were

             G                                D
               And into every masterpiece of literature

                          Asus4  D
             For dignity


             D                                       G      D
Verse 11     Englishman stranded in the blackheart wind

                                          G            D
             Combin' his hair back, his future looks thin

             G                          D
               Bites the bullet and he looks within

                          Asus4  D
             For dignity


             A
Bridge 4       Someone showed me a picture and I just laughed

             G                                   D
               Dignity never been photographed

               G                 D
             I went into the red, went into the black

             Em                                   A
               Into the valley of dry bone dreams


             D                           G      D
Verse 12     So many roads, so much at stake

                                            G           D
             So many dead ends, I'm at the edge of the lake

             G                        D
               Sometimes I wonder   what it's gonna take

                              Asus4  D
             To find dignity


Outro        |: D      | G  D   | D       | G       D   |

             | G       | D      | D       | Asus4  D  :|   Repeat to fade
```

DON'T THINK TWICE, IT'S ALL RIGHT

Words & Music by Bob Dylan

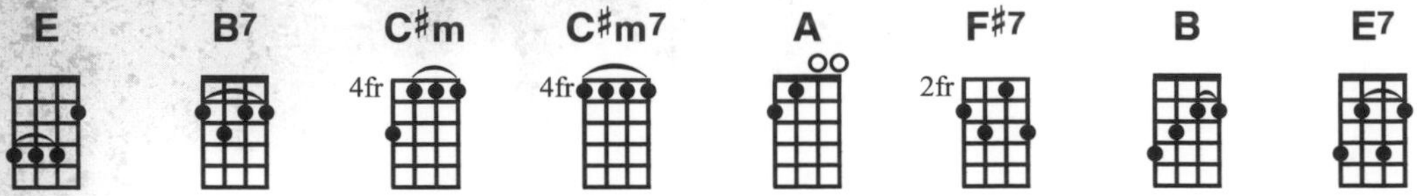

Intro | E B7 | C#m C#m7 A | E B7 | E ||

Verse 1

E B7 C#m C#m7
It ain't no use to sit and wonder why, babe
A E B7
It don't matter, anyhow
E B7 C#m C#m7
An' it ain't no use to sit and wonder why, babe
F#7 B7
If you don't know by now
E E7
When your rooster crows at the break of dawn
A F#7
Look out your window and I'll be gone
E B7 C#m C#m7 A
You're the reason I'm trav'lin' on
E B7 E
Don't think twice, it's all right

Link 1 | E B | C#m C#m7 | A | E | E ||

Verse 2

```
 E                B7                C#m       C#m7
It ain't no use in turnin' on your light, babe
     A          E       B7
The light I never knowed
        E               B7                 C#m        C#m7
An' it ain't no use in turnin' on your light, babe
F#7                              B7
   I'm on the dark side of the road
        E                                         E7
Still I wish there was somethin' you would   do or say
   A                                F#7
To try and make me change my mind and stay
    E      B7            C#m    C#m7     A
We never did too much talkin' anyway
   E            B7           E
So don't think twice, it's all right
```

Link 2

| E B | C#m C#m7 | A | E | E ||

Verse 3

```
 E                B7                C#m       C#m7
It ain't no use in callin' out my name, gal
A                                E       B7
   Like you never did before
 E                B7                C#m       C#m7
It ain't no use in callin' out my name, gal
F#7                             B7
   I can't hear you anymore
        E                                E7
I'm a-thinkin' and a-wond'rin' all the way down the road
  A                        F#7
I once loved a woman, a child I'm told
  E            B7          C#m     C#m7     A
I give her my heart but she wanted my soul
    E            B7            E
But don't think twice, it's all   right
```

Link 3

| E B7 | C#m C#m7 | A | E B7 | E | E ||

Verse 4

```
    E                 B7                C#m
I'm walkin' down that long, lonesome road, babe
C#m7        A             E    B7
Where I'm bound, I can't tell
    E            B7           C#m      C#m7
But goodbye's too good a word, gal
F#7                     B7
  So I'll just say fare thee well
E                           E7
I ain't sayin' you treated me unkind
    A                           F#7
You could have done better but  I don't mind
E              B7           C#m   C#m7  A
You just kinda wasted my   pre - cious   time
    E            B7          E
But don't think twice, it's all right
```

Coda

```
| E    B7  | C#m  C#m7      | A        | E        |
| E    B7  | C#m  C#m7      | F#7      | B    B7  |
| E        | E7             | A        | F#7      |
| E    B7  | C#m  C#m7   A  | E  B  B7 | E   A    | E      ||
```

DUQUESNE WHISTLE

Words by Bob Dylan & Rob Hunter
Music by Bob Dylan

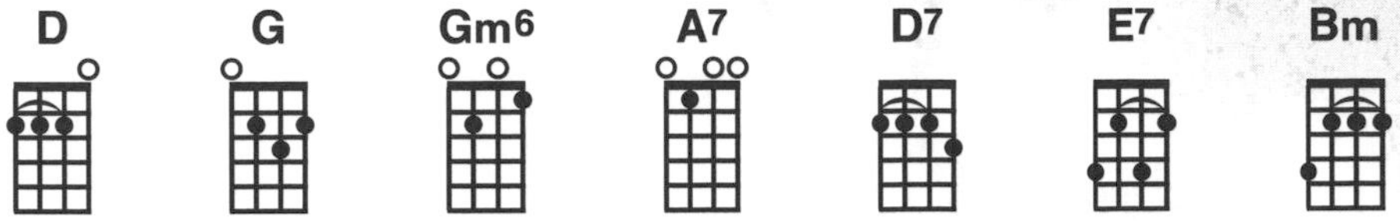

To match original recording, tune ukulele up a semitone

Intro

```
𝄆 D    | G    | D    | G  Gm6 |
| D    | D A7 | D    | D    𝄇
| D7   | D7   | G    | G    |
| D7   | D7   | A7   | A7   ||
𝄆 D    | G    | D    | G  Gm6 |
| D    | D A7 | D    | D    𝄇
```

Verse 1

```
D              G                    D          G   Gm6
Listen to that Duquesne whistle blowin'
D                                      A7      D
Blowin' like it's gonna sweep my world a - way
                       G                       D       G   Gm6
I'm gonna stop at Carbondale and keep on going
     D                                  A7       D
That Duquesne train gonna ride me night and day
D7                          G
You say I'm a gambler, you say I'm a pimp
E7                       A7
   But I ain't neither one
D              G          D                    G   Gm6
Listen to that Duquesne whistle blowin'
D                        A7  D
Sound like it's on a final run
```

Link 1

```
| G  D | D    | G  D | D    ||
```

Verse 2

D G D G Gm6
Listen to that Duquesne whistle blowin'
D A7 D
Blowin' like she never blowed be - fore
G D G Gm6
Blue light blinking, red light glowin'
D A7 D
Blowin' like she's at my chamber door
D7 G
You smiling through the fence at me
E7 A7
Just like you always smiled be - fore
D G D G Gm6
Listen to that Duquesne whistle blowin'
D A7 D
Blowin' like she ain't gonna blow no more

Link 2

| D | G | D | G Gm6 |
| D | D A7 | D | D ||

Verse 3

D G D G Gm6
Can't you hear that Duquesne whistle blowin'
D A7 D
Blowin' like the sky's gonna blow a - part
G D G Gm6
You're the only thing a - live that keeps me goin'
D A7 D
You're like a time bomb in my heart
D7 G
I can hear a sweet voice gently calling
E7 A7
Must be the Mother of our Lord
D G D G Gm6
Listen to that Duquesne whistle blowin'
D A7 D
Blowin' like my woman's on board

Link 3

| G D | D | G D | D ||

Verse 4

D G D G Gm6
Listen to that Duquesne whistle blowin'
D A7 D
Blowin' like it's gonna blow my blues a - way

cont.

```
                         G                        D       G  Gm6
You ole rascal, I know ex - actly where you're goin'
   D                                A7      D
I'll lead you there myself at the break of day
  D7                               G
I wake up every morning with that woman in my bed
E7                          A7
Everybody telling me she's gone to my head
D            G                   D         G  Gm6
Listen to that Duquesne whistle blowin'
D                        A7     D
Blowin' like it's gonna kill me dead
```

Link 4

D	A7	G	Bm
G	D	A7	A7
D	G	D	G Gm6
D	D A7	D	D	

Verse 5

```
D                    G                  D         G  Gm6
Can't you hear that Duquesne whistle blowin'
D                          A7      D
Blowin' through another no-good town
                  G              D          G  Gm6
The lights of my native land are glowin'
 D                              A7         D
I wonder if they'll know me next time a - round
D7                                G
I wonder if that old oak tree's still standing
    E7                                   A7
That old oak tree, the one we used to climb
D             G                   D         G  Gm6
Listen to that Duquesne whistle blowin'
D                            A7     D
Blowin' like she's blowin' right on time
```

Link 5

| A7 | A7 | A7 | A7 |
| A7 | A7 | A7 | A7 ||

Outro

|: D | G | D | G Gm6 |
| D | D A7 | D | D :| *Repeat to fade*

EVERY GRAIN OF SAND

Words & Music by Bob Dylan

To match original recording, tune ukulele up a semitone

Intro | D G | D G | D G | D G ||

Verse 1

D G D G
In the time of my confession, in the hour of my deepest need
D G A Asus4 A
When the pool of tears beneath my feet flood every newborn seed
D G D G
There's a dyin' voice within me reaching out somewhere
D G A Asus4 A
Toiling in the danger and in the morals of des - pair

Chorus 1

A A7 D A
Don't have the inclination to look back on any mistake
A7 D A G
Like Cain, I now behold this chain of events that I must break
D Gmaj9 D Gmaj9
In the fury of the moment I can see the Master's hand
D Gmaj9 A A7 D
In every leaf that trembles, in every grain of sand

Verse 2

D G D G
Oh, the flowers of indulgence and the weeds of yesteryear
D G A Asus4 A
Like criminals, they have choked the breath of conscience and good cheer
D G D G
The sun beat down upon the steps of time to light the way
D G A Asus4 A
To ease the pain of idleness and the memory of decay

Chorus 2

```
  A                A7                   D                A
I gaze into the doorway of temptation's angry flame
                     A7                 D                A        G
And every time I pass that way I always hear my name
      D               Gmaj9    D                Gmaj9
Then onward in my journey I come to understand
      D             Gmaj9            A      A7       D
That every hair is numbered like every grain of sand
```

Solo

```
|: D     G    | D     G    | D     G    | A  Asus4  A :|
|  A     A7   | D     A    | A     A7   | D      A  G  |
|  D   Gmaj9  | D   Gmaj9  | D   Gmaj9  | A  A7  D     ||
```

Verse 3

```
       D                    G              D                 G
I have gone from rags to riches in the sorrow of the night
       D          G                         A          Asus4   A
In the violence of a summer's dream, in the chill of a wintry  light
       D              G          D          G
In the bitter dance of loneliness fading into space
       D                 G               A          Asus4  A
In the broken mirror of innocence on each forgotten  face
```

Chorus 3

```
  A                A7                   D              A
I hear the ancient footsteps like the motion of the sea
                           A7                     D             A      G
Sometimes I turn, there's someone there, other times it's only me
     D                        Gmaj9  D                 Gmaj9
I am hanging in the balance   of the reality of man
     D               Gmaj9         A      A7       D
Like every sparrow falling, like every grain of sand
```

Coda

```
|: D     G    | D     G    | D     G    | A  Asus4  A :|
|  A     A7   | D     A    | A     A7   | D      A  G  |
|  D   Gmaj9  | D   Gmaj9  | D   Gmaj9  | A  A7  D     ||
```

EVERYTHING IS BROKEN

Words & Music by Bob Dylan

E7 A7 B7

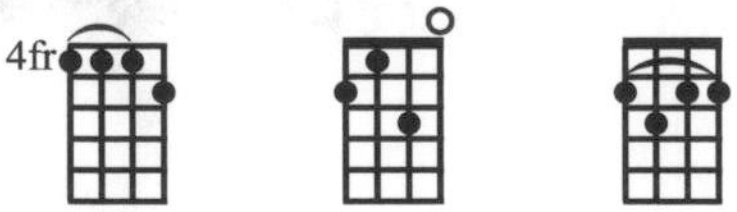

Intro ‖: E7 | E7 | E7 | E7 :‖

Verse 1

E7
Broken lines, broken strings
Broken threads, broken springs
A7
Broken idols, broken heads
E7
People sleeping in broken beds
B7
Ain't no use jiving
A7
Ain't no use joking
E7
Everything is broken

Link 1 | E7 | E7 | E7 | E7 ‖

Verse 2

E7
Broken bottles, broken plates
Broken switches, broken gates
A7
Broken dishes, broken parts
E7
Streets are filled with broken hearts
B7   A7
Broken words never meant to be spoken
E7
Everything is broken

Link 2 As Link 1

Bridge 1

B7
Seem like every time you stop and turn around
A7
Something else just hit the ground

Verse 3

E7
Broken cutters, broken saws

Broken buckles, broken laws
A7
Broken bodies, broken bones
E7
Broken voices on broken phones
B7 A7
Take a deep breath, feel like you're chokin'
E7
Everything is broken

Instrumental

E7	E7	E7	E7
A7	A7	E7	E7
B7	A7	E7	E7	

Bridge 2

B7
Every time you leave and go off someplace
A7
Things fall to pieces in my face

Verse 4

E7
Broken hands on broken ploughs

Broken treaties, broken vows
A7
Broken pipes, broken tools
E7
People bending broken rules
B7 A7
Hound dog howling, bullfrog croaking
E7
Everything is broken

Outro

||: E7 | E7 | E7 | E7 |
| A7 | A7 | E7 | E7 |
| B7 | A7 | E7 | E7 :|| *Repeat and fade*

FOREVER YOUNG

Words & Music by Bob Dylan

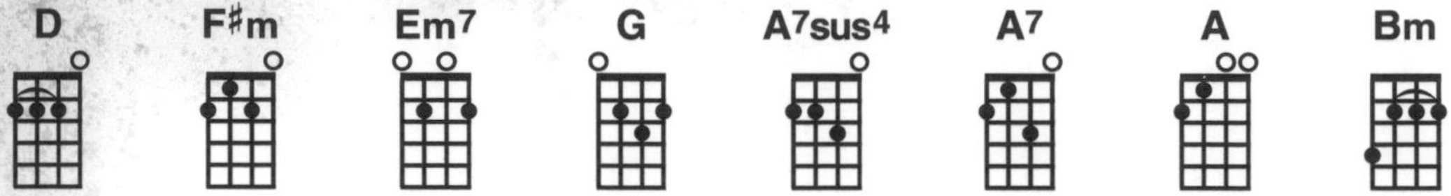

Intro | D | D | D | D ||

Verse 1

```
             D
May God bless and keep you always
              F♯m
May your wishes all come true
             Em7
May you always do for others
          G                  D
And let others do for you
May you build a ladder to the stars
      F♯m
And climb on every rung
               Em7   A7sus4   A7      D
May you stay                   forever young
```

Chorus 1

```
               A       Bm
Forever young, forever young
             D     A        D
May you   stay__ forever young
```

Verse 2

```
             D
May you grow up to be righteous
                 F♯m
May you grow up to be true
             Em7
May you always know the truth
                G                    D
And see the lights surrounding you
```

cont.

May you always be courageous

F♯m
Stand upright and be strong

Em7 A7sus4 A7 D
May you stay forever young

A Bm
Chorus 2 Forever young, forever young

D A D
May you stay____ forever young

D
Verse 3 May your hands always be busy

F♯m
May your feet always be swift

G
May you have a strong foundation

D
When the winds of changes shift

May your heart always be joyful

F♯m
May your song always be sung

G A7sus4 A7 D
May you stay forever young

A Bm
Chorus 3 Forever young, forever young

D A D
May you stay___ forever young

Coda

| D | F♯m | G | G | D | D |

| D | F♯m | G | A | D | D |

| A | A | Bm | Bm |

| D | A | D | D ||

GIRL FROM THE NORTH COUNTRY

Words & Music by Bob Dylan

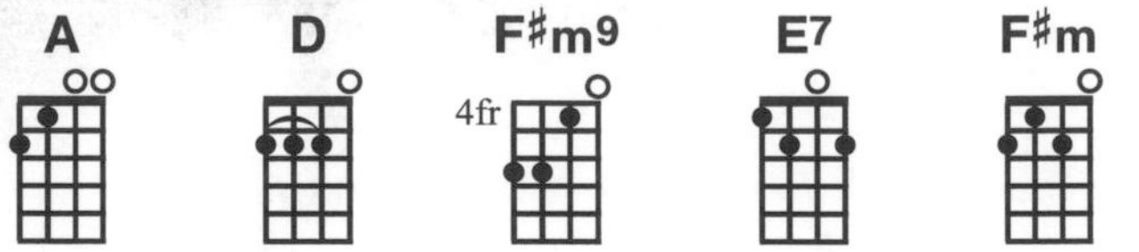

To match original recording, tune ukulele up a semitone

Intro | A | D | D A | D A | D A | A | A |

```
Verse 1   F♯m9                              E7          A   D A
          Well, if you're travelin' in the north   country fair
                   F♯m9                          E7         A    D A
          Where the winds hit heavy on the bor - derline
              F♯m              D              A   D A
          Re - member me to one who lives there
          F♯m9          E7          A   D A
          She once was a true love of mine

Verse 2   F♯m9                         E7          A   D A
          Well, if you go when the snowflakes storm
                   F♯m9             E7          A   D A
          When the rivers freeze and     summer ends
              F♯m                        D       A   D A
          Please   see if she's wearing a coat so warm
             F♯m9                    E7   D A          E7    A
          To keep her from the howl  -  in' winds

Verse 3   F♯m9                         E7          A   D A
             Please see for me if her hair hangs long
             F♯m9              E7          A   D A
          If it rolls and flows all    down her breast
              F♯m                  D         A   D A
          Please   see for me if her hair hangs long
          F♯m9               E7          A   D A
          That's the way I re - member her best
```

Verse 4

```
              F♯m9                  E7               A   D   A
I'm a - wonderin' if she re - members me at all
F♯m9                 E7        A   D   A
Many times I've      often prayed
F♯m                  D     A   D   A
In the darkness of my night
F♯m9                 E7      A   D   A
In the brightness of my day
```

Harmonica solo

```
|: F♯m9  | F♯m9  | E7    | A     | A     :|
|  F♯m   | F♯m   | D     | A     | A     |
|  F♯m9  | F♯m9  | E7    | A     | D     | A     | A     |
```

Verse 5

```
        F♯m9                    E7               A   D   A
So if you're travelin' in the north country fair
              F♯m9                      E7         A   D   A
Where the winds hit heavy on the borderline
       F♯m             D                 A   D   A
Re - member me to one who lives there
F♯m9                E7          D   A
She once was a true love of mine
```

Harmonica outro

```
| F♯m9  | F♯m9  | F♯m9  | F♯m9  | F♯m9  | F♯m9  | F♯m9  |
| E7    | E7    | E7    | E7    | A     | D     | A     ||
```

GOTTA SERVE SOMEBODY

Words & Music by Bob Dylan

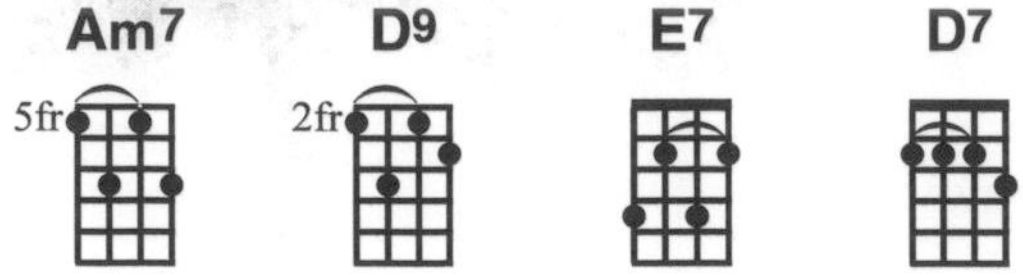

Intro | (Am7) | (Am7) | (Am7) | (Am7) ||

Verse 1

Am7
You may be an ambassador to England or France

You may like to gamble, you might like to dance

You may be the heavyweight champion of the world

You may be a socialite with a long string of pearls

D9
But you're gonna have to serve somebody, yes indeed

Am7
You're gonna have to serve somebody

E7 D9 E7
Well, it may be the devil or it may be the Lord

D7 Am7
But you're gonna have to serve somebody

Verse 2

Am7
You might be a rock 'n' roll addict prancing on the stage

You might have drugs at your command, women in a cage

You may be a businessman or some high-degree thief

They may call you Doctor or they may call you Chief

D9
But you're gonna have to serve somebody, yes indeed

Am7
You're gonna have to serve somebody

E7 D9
Well, it may be the devil or it may be the Lord

E7 D7 Am7
But you're gonna have to serve somebody

Verse 3

Am7
You may be a state trooper, you might be a young Turk

You may be the head of some big TV network

You may be rich or poor, you may be blind or lame

You may be living in another country under another name

D9
But you're gonna have to serve somebody, yes indeed

Am7
You're gonna have to serve somebody

E7 **D9**
Well, it may be the devil or it may be the Lord

E7 **D7** **Am7**
But you're gonna have to serve somebody

Verse 4

Am7
You may be a construction worker working on a home

You may be living in a mansion or you might live in a dome

You might own guns and you might even own tanks

You might be somebody's landlord, you might even own banks

D9
But you're gonna have to serve somebody, yes indeed

Am7
You're gonna have to serve somebody

E7 **D9** **E7**
Well, it may be the devil or it may be the Lord

D7 **Am7**
But you're gonna have to serve somebody

Verse 5

Am7
You may be a preacher with your spiritual pride

You may be a city councilman taking bribes on the side

You may be workin' in a barbershop, you may know how to cut hair

You may be somebody's mistress, may be somebody's heir

cont.

D9
But you're gonna have to serve somebody, yes indeed
Am7
You're gonna have to serve somebody
E7 D9
Well, it may be the devil or it may be the Lord
E7 D7 Am7
But you're gonna have to serve somebody

Verse 6

Am7
Might like to wear cotton, might like to wear silk

Might like to drink whiskey, might like to drink milk

You might like to eat caviar, you might like to eat bread

You may be sleeping on the floor, sleeping in a king-sized bed
D9
But you're gonna have to serve somebody, yes indeed
Am7
You're gonna have to serve somebody
E7 D9
Well, it may be the devil or it may be the Lord
E7 D7 Am7
But you're gonna have to serve somebody

Verse 7

Am7
You may call me Terry, you may call me Timmy

You may call me Bobby, you may call me Zimmy

You may call me R.J., you may call me Ray

You may call me anything but no matter what you say
D9
You're gonna have to serve somebody, yes indeed
Am7
You're gonna have to serve somebody
E7 D9 E7
Well, it may be the devil or it may be the Lord
D7 Am7
But you're gonna have to serve somebody

Coda 𝄆 Am7 | Am7 | Am7 | Am7 𝄇 *Repeat to fade*

A HARD RAIN'S A-GONNA FALL

Words & Music by Bob Dylan

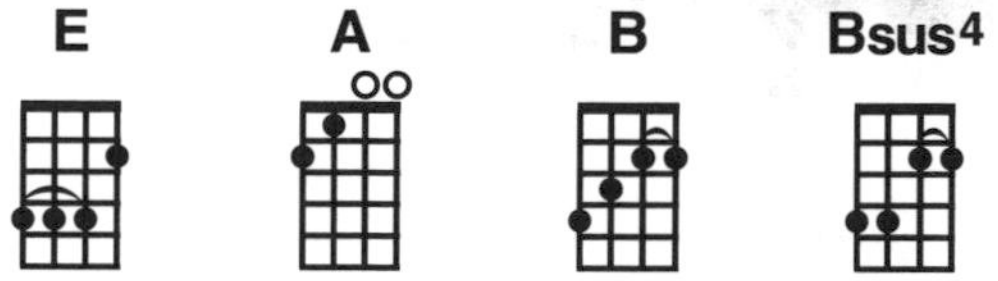

Intro | E A E | E ||

Verse 1

```
      E                              A         E
Oh, where have you been, my blue-eyed son?
                                                 B
Oh, where have you been, my darling young one?
     A                            Bsus4          E
I've stumbled on the side of twelve misty mountains
            A                           Bsus4       E
I've walked   and I've crawled on six crooked highways
            A                      Bsus4      E
I've stepped   in the middle of seven sad forests
     A                          Bsus4        E
I've been out in front of a dozen dead oceans
            A                              Bsus4       E
I've been ten thousand miles in the mouth of a graveyard
                          B               E                 A
And it's a hard, and it's a hard, it's a hard, and it's a hard
             E            B              E     A  E
And it's a hard rain's______ a-gonna fall
```

Verse 2

```
      E                       A          E
Oh, what did you see, my blue-eyed son?
                                             B
Oh, what did you see, my darling young one?
         A                             Bsus4          E
I saw a newborn baby with wild wolves all around it
            A                             Bsus4  E
I saw a highway of diamonds with nobody on it
       A                      Bsus4            E
I saw a black branch with blood that kept drippin'
```

```
                       A                               Bsus4      E
cont.       I saw a room full of men with their hammers a-bleedin'
                 A                 Bsus4            E
            I saw a white ladder all covered with water
                   A                          Bsus4          E
            I saw ten thousand talkers whose tongues were all broken
                    A                            Bsus4          E
            I saw guns and sharp swords in the hands of young children
                                      B         E          A
            And it's a hard, and it's a hard, it's a hard, it's a hard
                    E            B            E    A  E
            And it's a hard rain's______ a-gonna fall

                E                        A        E
Verse 3     And what did you hear, my blue-eyed son?
                                                   B
            And what did you hear, my darling young one?
                    A                        Bsus4       E
            I heard the sound of a thunder, it roared out a warnin'
                   A                             Bsus4          E
            Heard the roar of a wave that could drown the whole world
                    A                               Bsus4        E
            Heard one hundred drummers whose hands were a-blazin'
                    A                            Bsus4  E
            Heard ten thousand whisperin' and nobody listenin'
                    A                         Bsus4           E
            Heard one person starve, I heard many people laughin'
                        A                Bsus4      E
            Heard the song of a poet who died in the gutter
                         A                 Bsus4       E
            Heard the sound of a clown who cried in the alley
                                      B         E     A
            And it's a hard, and it's a hard, it's a hard, it's a hard
                E           B               E    A  E
            It's a hard rain's______ a-gonna fall

                E                       A        E
Verse 4     Oh, who did you meet, my blue-eyed son?
                                                 B
            Who did you meet, my darling young one?
                A              Bsus4       E
            I met a young child beside a dead pony
                  A              Bsus4          E
            I met a white man who walked a black dog
```

cont.

```
        A                 Bsus4    E
I met a young woman whose body was burning
        A               Bsus4     E
I met a young girl, she gave me a rainbow
      A               Bsus4   E
I met one man who was wounded in love
      A                   Bsus4   E
I met another man who was wounded with hatred
                        B            E            A
And it's a hard, it's a hard, it's a hard, it's a hard
       E            B           E    A  E
It's a hard rain's______ a-gonna fall
```

Verse 5

```
    E                      A         E   A  E
Oh, what'll you do now, my blue-eyed son?
                                         B
Oh, what'll you do now, my darling young one?
            A                 Bsus4        E
I'm a-goin' back out 'fore the rain starts a-fallin'
           A                    Bsus4         E
I'll walk to the depths of the deepest black forest
                 A                  Bsus4         E
Where the people are many and their hands are all empty
          A                    Bsus4          E
Where the pellets of poison are flooding their waters
               A                       Bsus4      E
Where the home in the valley meets the damp dirty prison
             A                  Bsus4       E
Where the executioner's face is always well hidden
             A              Bsus4      E
Where hunger is ugly, where souls are forgotten
            A                   Bsus4    E
Where black is the color, where none is the number
              A                   Bsus4               E
And I'll tell it and speak it and think it and breathe it
               A                      Bsus4         E
And reflect it from the mountain so all souls can see it
                A                 Bsus4   E
Then I'll stand on the ocean until I start sinkin'
         A                          Bsus4 E
But I'll know my song well before I start singin'
                        B            E            A
And it's a hard, it's a hard, it's a hard, it's a hard
       E            B           E    A  E
It's a hard rain's______ a-gonna fall
```

HIGH WATER (FOR CHARLEY PATTON)

Words & Music by Bob Dylan

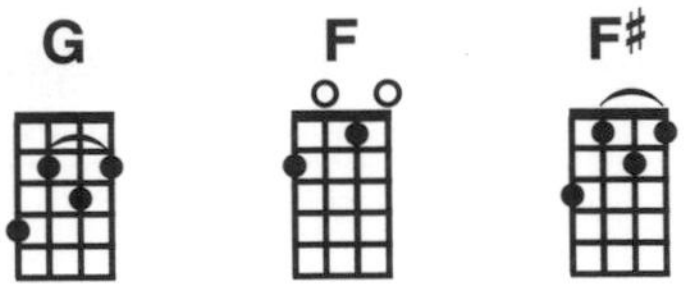

Intro | G | G F F♯ | G | G F5 F♯ |
| G | G ||

Verse 1

G
High water risin' – risin' night and day
All the gold and silver are being stolen away
Big Joe Turner lookin' East and West
From the dark room of his mind
He made it to Kansas City
Twelfth Street and Vine
F F♯ G
Nothing standing there
F F♯ G
High water every - where.

Verse 2

G
High water risin', the shacks are slidin' down
Folks losin' their possessions – folks are leaving town
Bertha Mason shook it – broke it
Then she hung it on the wall
Says, "You're dancin' with whom they tell you to
Or you don't dance at all."

```
          F            F#         G
cont.     It's rough out      there
              F       F#         G
          High water every - where.

          G
Verse 3   I got a cravin' love for blazing speed

          Got a hopped-up Mustang Ford

          Jump into the wagon, baby, throw your panties overboard

          I can write you poems, make a strong man lose his mind

          I'm no pig without a wig

          I hope you treat me kind
                          F            F#      G
          Things are breakin' up out there
              F       F#         G
          High water every - where.

          G
Verse 4   High water risin', six inches 'bove my head

          Coffins droppin' in the street

          Like balloons made out of lead

          Water pourin' into Vicksburg, don't know what I'm going to do

          "Don't reach out for me," she said

          "Can't you see I'm drownin' too?"
              F              F#   G
          It's dark out      there
              F       F#         G
          High water every - where

          G
Verse 5   George Lewis told the Englishman, the Italian and the Jew

          "You can't open up your mind, boys

          To every conceivable point of view"
```

```
cont.       They got Charles Darwin trapped out there on Highway Five

            Judge says to the High Sheriff

            "I want him dead or alive
            F             F♯      G
            Either one, I don't care."
                   F       F♯       G
            High water every - where

Verse 6     The Cuckoo is a pretty bird, she warbles as she flies

            I'm preachin' the Word of God

            I'm puttin' out your eyes

            I asked Fat Nancy for something to eat, she said, "Take it off the shelf –

            As great as you are a man

            You'll never be greater than yourself."
                          F       F♯      G
            I told her I didn't really care
                   F       F♯       G
            High water every - where
            G
Verse 7     I'm gettin' up in the morning – I believe I'll dust my broom

            I'm keeping away from the women, I'm givin' 'em lots of room

            Thunder rolling over Clarkesdale, everything is looking blue

            I just can't be happy, love

            Unless you're happy too
                F    F♯  G
            It's bad out there
                   F       F♯       G
            High water every - where

Outro       | G        | G        | G        | G        |

            | G        | G        | G        | G        |

            | G  F  F♯ | G  F  F♯ | G        ‖  To fade
```

I BELIEVE IN YOU

Words & Music by Bob Dylan

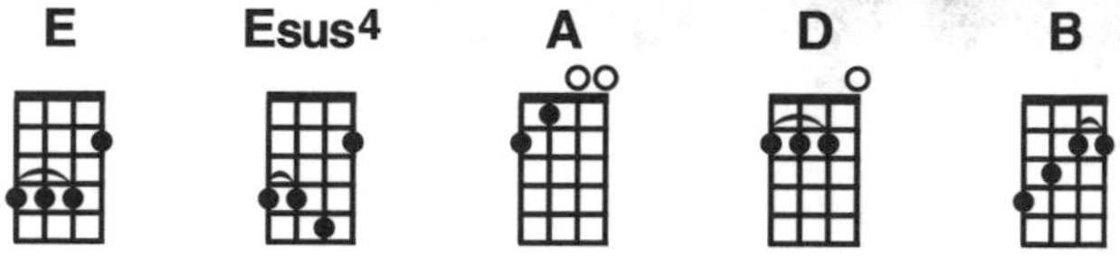

Intro | E Esus4 E Esus4 E | E Esus4 E Esus4 E | E ‖

Verse 1

```
E
They ask me how I feel

And if my love is real
                    A       E
And how I know I'll make it through
               A       E
And they, they look at me and frown
                                  D
They'd like to drive me from this town
                       A
They don't want me a - round
              E
'Cause I be - lieve in you
```

Verse 2

```
E
They show me to the door

They say don't come back no more
                              A       E
'Cause I don't be like they'd like me to
               A     E
And I walk out on my own
                      D
A thousand miles from home
                     A
But I don't feel a - lone
              E
'Cause I be - lieve in you
```

Chorus 1

```
            D           A                       E
I be - lieve in you even through the tears and the laughter
            D           A                   E      Esus4 E
I be - lieve in you even though we be a - part
            D           A                   E
I be - lieve in you even on the morning af - ter
A                B     E       A
Oh, when the dawn is near - ing
                 B     E         A
Oh, when the night is disap - pearing
         B          E         A     B
Oh, this feeling is still here in my heart
```

Verse 3

```
E
Don't let me drift too far

Keep me where you are
                           A       E
Where I will always be re - newed
                     A       E
And that which you've given me today
                                D
Is worth more than I could pay
                               A
And no matter what they say
     E
I be - lieve in you
```

Instrumental

```
| E   Esus4 E Esus4 E | E   Esus4 E Esus4 E |
| E   Esus4 E Esus4 E | A         | E         |
| E   Esus4 E Esus4 E | E   Esus4 E Esus4 E |
| D       | A         | E         | E         ||
```

Chorus 2

```
        D                 A           E
I be - lieve in you when winter turn to summer
        D                 A          E
I be - lieve in you when white turn to black
        D           A                   E
I be - lieve in you even though I be out - numbered
A                 B     E       A
Oh, though the earth may shake me
                  B     E    A
Oh, though my friends forsake me
          B  E       A      B
Oh, even that couldn't make me go back
```

Verse 4

```
E
Don't let me change my heart

Keep me set apart
                              A     E
From all the plans they do pur - sue

And I, I don't mind the pain
                             D
Don't mind the driving rain
                        A
I know I will sus - tain
                E
'Cause I be - lieve in you
```

Outro

```
||: E   Esus4 E Esus4 E | E   Esus4 E Esus4 E |
|   E   Esus4 E Esus4 E | A        | E        |
|   E   Esus4 E Esus4 E | E   Esus4 E Esus4 E |
|   D        | A        | E       :||
```

Repeat to fade

HURRICANE

Words & Music by Bob Dylan & Jacques Levy

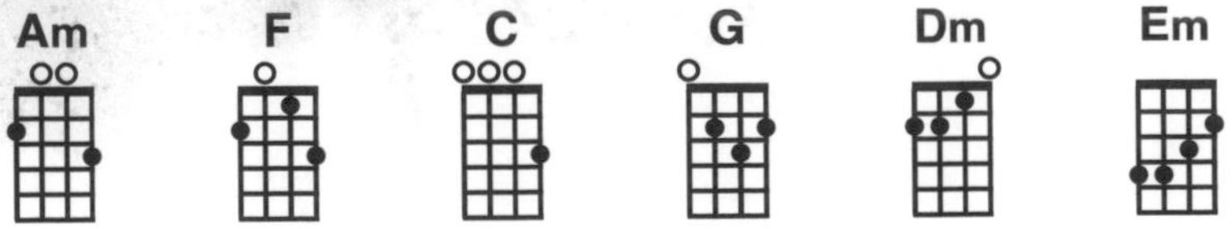


```
Intro      |: Am    | F     | Am    | F    :|

           Am                        F
Verse 1     Pistol shots ring out in the barroom night
           Am                             F
           Enter Patty Valentine from the upper hall
           Am                           F
              She sees the bartender in a pool of blood
           Am                         F
              Cries out, "My God, they killed them all!"

           C  N.C.                         F  N.C.    G
Chorus 1      Here comes the story of the Hurricane
           C  N.C.                     F  N.C.        G
              The man the authorities came to blame
           Dm                            C
              For somethin' that he never done
           Dm                         C    Em              Am
              Put in a prison cell, but one time he could-a been
               F                C        G
            The champion of the world

Link 1     | Am    | F     | Am    | F     ||

           Am                               F
Verse 2       Three bodies lyin' there does Patty see
               Am                                   F
            And another man named Bello, movin' around mysteriously
           Am                                  F
              "I didn't do it," he says, and he throws up his hands
                  Am                           F
            "I was only robbin' the register, I hope you understand
```

```
            C  N.C.                       F  N.C.            G
Chorus 2      I saw them leavin'," he says, and he stops
            C   N.C.                     F  N.C.        G
              "One of us had better call up the cops"
            Dm                       C
              And so Patty calls the cops
            Dm                        C                Em       Am
              And they arrive on the scene with their red lights flashin'
                 F                  C     G
            In the hot New Jersey night


Link 2      | Am      | F       | Am      | F       ||


            Am                          F
Verse 3     Meanwhile, far away in another part of town
            Am                                      F
            Rubin Carter and a couple of friends are drivin' around
            Am                              F
            Number one contender for the middleweight crown
                 Am                       F
            Had no idea what kinda shit was about to go down


            C  N.C.                                 F  N.C.         G
Chorus 3      When a cop pulled him over to the side of the road
            C  N.C.                               F  N.C.         G
              Just like the time before and the time before that
              Dm                                  C
            In Paterson that's just the way things   go
                        Dm                        C     Em      Am
            If you're black you might as well not show up on the street
                         F                 C     G
            'Less you wanna draw the heat


Link 3      | Am      | F       | Am      | F       ||


            Am                                      F
Verse 4     Alfred Bello had a partner and he had a rap for the cops
            Am                                            F
            Him and Arthur Dexter Bradley were just out   prowlin' around
               Am                                      F
            He said, "I saw two men runnin' out, they looked like middleweights
                 Am                           F
            They jumped into a white car with out-of-state plates"
```

```
Chorus 4   C  N.C.                          F  N.C.          G
             And Miss Patty Valentine just nodded her head
           C          N.C.                  F  N.C.           G
           Cop said, "Wait a minute, boys, this one's not dead"
                 Dm                         C
           So they took him to the infirmary
           Dm                                     C
             And though this man could hardly see
                Em                    Am    F          C      G
           They told him that he could identify the guilty men

Link 4     | Am      | F        | Am       | F        ||

           Am                               F
Verse 5      Four in the mornin' and they haul Rubin in
           Am                                 F
           Take him to the hospital and they bring him upstairs
               Am                                  F
           The wounded man looks up through his one dyin' eye
                 Am                               F
           Says, "Wha'd you bring him in here for? He ain't the guy!"

           C  N.C.                       F  N.C.         G
Chorus 5     Yes, here's the story of the   Hurricane
           C  N.C.                    F  N.C.          G
             The man the authorities came to blame
           Dm                                C
             For somethin' that he never done
           Dm                          C   Em              Am
             Put in a prison cell, but one time he could-a been
               F                  C       G
           The champion of the world

Link 5     | Am      | F        | Am       | F        ||

           Am                          F
Verse 6      Four months later, the ghettos are in flame
           Am                              F
           Rubin's in South America, fightin' for his name
                Am                                    F
           While Arthur Dexter Bradley's still in the robbery game
                  Am                                                    F
           And the cops are puttin' the screws to him, lookin' for somebody to blame
```

Chorus 6

```
C  N.C.                           F  N.C.         G
  "Remember that murder that happened in a bar?"
C  N.C.                             F  N.C.      G
"Remember you said you saw the getaway car?"
     Dm                               C
"You think you'd like to play ball with the law?"
Dm                                             C    Em        Am
"Think it might-a been that fighter that you saw runnin' that night?"
        F              C       G
"Don't forget that you are white"
```

Link 6

| Am | F | Am | F ||

Verse 7

```
Am                             F
Arthur Dexter Bradley said, "I'm really not sure"
Am                                     F
Cops said, "A poor boy like you could use a break
   Am                              F
We got you for the motel job and we're talkin' to your friend Bello
    Am                                    F
Now you don't wanta have to go back to jail, be a nice fellow
```

Chorus 7

```
C  N.C.             F  N.C.       G
  You'll be doin' society a favor
C  N.C.                F  N.C.              G
  That sonofabitch is brave and getting braver
Dm                         C
  We want to put his ass in stir
Dm                         C    Em     Am
  We want to pin this triple murder on him
   F                 C      G
He ain't no Gentleman Jim"
```

Link 7

| Am | F | Am | F ||

Verse 8

```
Am                              F
Rubin could take a man out with just one punch
        Am                           F
But he never did like to talk about it all that much
        Am                F
It's my work, he'd say, and I do it for pay
Am                                F
  And when it's over I'd just as soon go on my way
```

Chorus 8

C N.C.   F N.C.   G
Up to some paradise
C N.C.   F N.C.   G
Where the trout streams flow and the air is nice
Dm   C
And ride a horse along a trail
Dm   C   Em
But then they took him to the jailhouse
          Am   F   C   G
Where they try to turn a man into a mouse

Link 8

| Am | F | Am | F ||

Verse 9

Am   F
All of Rubin's cards were marked in advance
   Am   F
The trial was a pig-circus, he never had a chance
   Am   F
The judge made Rubin's witnesses drunkards from the slums
     Am   F
To the white folks who watched he was a revolutionary bum

Chorus 9

C N.C.   F N.C.   G
And to the black folks he was just a crazy nigger
C N.C.   F N.C.   G
No one doubted that he pulled the trigger
Dm   C
And though they could not produce the gun
Dm   C   Em   Am
The D.A. said he was the one who did the deed
       F   C   G
And the all-white jury agreed

Link 9

| Am | F | Am | F ||

Verse 10

Am   F
Rubin Carter was falsely tried
   Am   F
The crime was murder "one," guess who testified?
Am   F
Bello and Bradley and they both baldly lied
       Am   F
And the newspapers, they all went along for the ride

```
              C   N.C.                    F  N.C.     G
Chorus 10        How can the life of such a man
              C   N.C.                 F  N.C.           G
                 Be in the palm of some fool's hand?
              Dm                          C
                 To see him obviously framed
              Dm                                   C        Em        Am
                 Couldn't help but make me feel ashamed to live in a land
                    F           C        G
              Where justice is a game


Link 10       | Am      | F        | Am      | F        ||


                   Am                          F
Verse 11      Now all the criminals in their coats and their ties
                  Am                            F
              Are free to drink martinis and watch the sun rise
                    Am                              F
              While Rubin sits like Buddha in a ten-foot cell
                 Am                 F
              An innocent man in a living hell


              C   N.C.                       F  N.C.     G
Chorus 11        That's the story of the Hurricane
              C   N.C.                              F  N.C.      G
                 But it won't be over till they clear his name
              Dm                                C
                 And give him back the time he's   done
              Dm                          C    Em            Am
                 Put in a prison cell, but one time he could-a been
                 F                C        G
              The champion of the world


Coda          | Am      | F        | Am      | F        |

              | Am      | F        | Am      | F        |

              | C       | F        | C       | F        |

              | Dm      | C        | Dm      | C   Em   |

              | Am   F  | C        | G       ||

              ||: Am    | F        | Am      | F       :||   Repeat to fade
```

I AND I

Words & Music by Bob Dylan

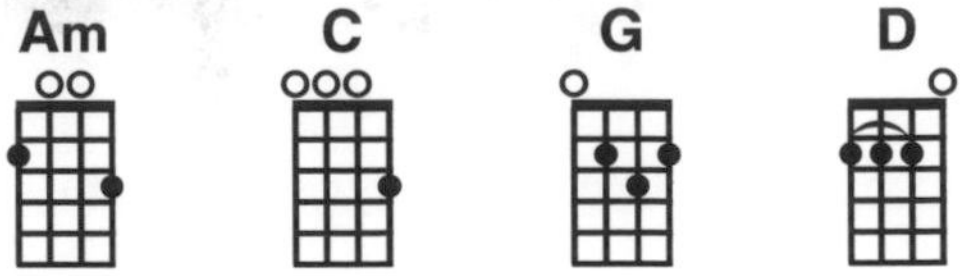

Intro

| Am C | G | D | Am ||

```
           Am                     C                         G
*Verse 1*  Been so long since a strange woman has slept in my bed
           D                           Am
            Look how sweet she sleeps, how free must be her dreams
                         C
           In another lifetime she must have owned the world, or been faithfully wed
           G                   D                        Am
           To some righteous king who wrote psalms beside moonlit streams
```

```
*Chorus 1* I and I
               G                   D              Am
           In creation where one's nature neither honors nor forgives

           I and I
           G                D            Am
           One says to the other, no man sees my face and lives
```

```
            Am        C            G
*Verse 2*  Think I'll go out and go for a walk
           D                         Am
           Not much happenin' here, nothin' ever does
                                   C              G
           Besides, if she wakes up now, she'll just want me to talk
           D                             Am
           I got nothin' to say, 'specially about whatever was
```

Chorus 2 As Chorus 1

Verse 3

```
  Am                    C                           G
Took an untrodden path once, where the swift don't win the race
D                                         Am
It goes to the worthy, who can divide the word of truth
                         C                           G
Took a stranger to teach me, to look into justice's beautiful face
D                                            Am
And to see an eye for an eye and a tooth for a tooth
```

Chorus 3 As Chorus 1

Verse 4

```
  Am                    C                                    G
Outside of two men on a train platform there's nobody in sight
D                                              Am
They're waiting for spring to come, smoking down the track
                                      C                    G
The world could come to an end tonight, but that's all right
D                                                          Am
She should still be there sleepin' when I get back
```

Chorus 4 As Chorus 1

Verse 5

```
Am                      C                                      G
Noontime, and I'm still pushin' myself along the road, the darkest part
D                                     Am
Into the narrow lanes, I can't stumble or stay put
                       C                                         G
Someone else is speakin' with my mouth, but I'm listening only to my heart
D                                                              Am
I've made shoes for everyone, even you, while I still go barefoot
```

Chorus 5 As Chorus 1

Outro 𝄆 Am | Am | Am | Am 𝄇 *Repeat to fade*

I DON'T BELIEVE YOU (SHE ACTS LIKE WE NEVER HAVE MET)

Words & Music by Bob Dylan

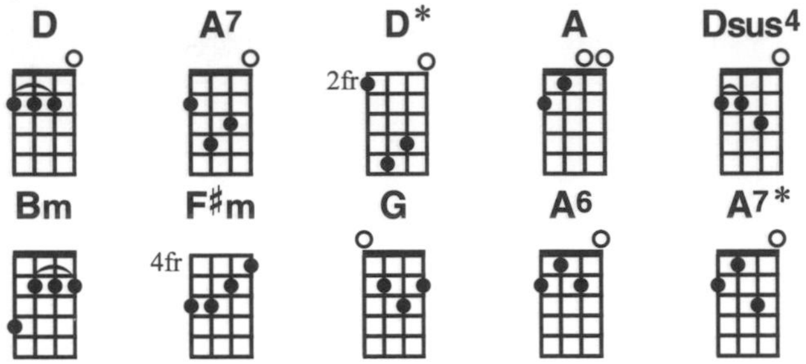

Intro | D* A7 | D A | D | D ||

Verse 1

```
 D*                A7
I can't under - stand
           D*         A7
She let go of my hand
      D*              A7             D       Dsus4  D
An' left me here facing the wall
    D*             A7
I'd sure like t' know
  D*              A7
Why she did go
     D*             A7                  D      Dsus4  D
But I can't get close t' her at all
                   Bm                                   F♯m
Though we kissed through the wild blazing nighttime
            G                          A
She said she would never for - get
A6      A7*   D*            A7
   But now mornin's clear
     D*             A7
It's like I ain't here
               D*              A7               D      Dsus4  D
She just acts like we never have met
```

Instrumental 1 | Bm | F♯m | G | A A6 A7* |

| D* A7 | D* A7 | D* A7 | D Dsus4 | D | D ||

Verse 2

```
   D*          A7
It's all new t' me
     D*              A7
Like some myste - ry
  D*             A7          D       Dsus4   D
It could even be like a myth
         D*              A7
Yet it's hard t' think on
      D*              A7
That she's the same one
D*        A7              D      Dsus4   D
That last night I was with
         Bm                               F♯m
From darkness, dreams're de - serted
        G                  A     A6    A7*
Am I still dreamin' yet?
 D*                  A7          D*                   A7
I wish she'd un - lock, her voice once an' talk
             D*              A7                    D       Dsus4   D
'Stead of acting like we never have met
```

Instrumental 2 | Bm | F♯m | D* A7 Bm | A A6 A7* |

| D* A7 | D* A7 | D* A7 | D Dsus4 | D | D ||

Verse 3

```
        D*               A7
If she ain't feelin' well
       D*                A7
Then why don't she tell
             D*              A7             D        Dsus4   D
'Stead of turnin' her back t' my face?
         D*          A7
With - out any doubt
     D*                 A7
She seems too far out
     D*            A7          D           Dsus4   D
For me t' re - turn t' her chase
                   Bm                          F♯m
Though the night ran swirling an' whirling
       G                               A      A6
I re - member her whispering yet
    A7*  D*             A7              D*           A7
But evi - dently she don't, an' evi - dently she won't
           A     A6         A7             D
She just acts like we never have met
```

Instrumental 3 As Instrumental 1

Verse 4

```
     D*             A7
If I didn't have t' guess
    D*           A7
I'd gladly con - fess
   D*       A7         D     Dsus4  D
T' anything I might've tried
         D*           A7
If I was with 'er too long
        D*             A7
Or have done something wrong
             D*              A7               D     Dsus4  D
I wish she'd tell me what it is, I'll run an' hide
           Bm                   F♯m
Though her skirt it swayed as a guitar played
    G                    A   A6
Her mouth was watery and wet
    A7* D*            A7           D*            A7
But now something has changed, for she ain't the same
         D*           A7         D      Dsus4  D
She just acts like we never have met
```

Instrumental 4 As Instrumental 1

Verse 5

```
    D*           A7
I'm leavin' to - day
     D*       A7
I'll be on my way
   D*           A7       D      Dsus4  D
Of this I can't say very much
       D*          A7
But if you want me to
      D*           A7
I can be just like you
          D*           A7         D
An' pre - tend that we never have touched
       Bm      F♯m
An' if anybody asks me
       G             A    A6
“Is it easy to for - get?”
     A7*        D*     A7            D*         A7
I'll say, “It's easily done, you just pick any - one
          D*            A7         D
An' pre - tend that you never have met!”
```

Outro

```
| Bm       | F♯m      | G        | A  A6  A7* |
| D*  A7   | D*  A7   | D*  A7   | D          ‖
```

I WANT YOU

Words & Music by Bob Dylan

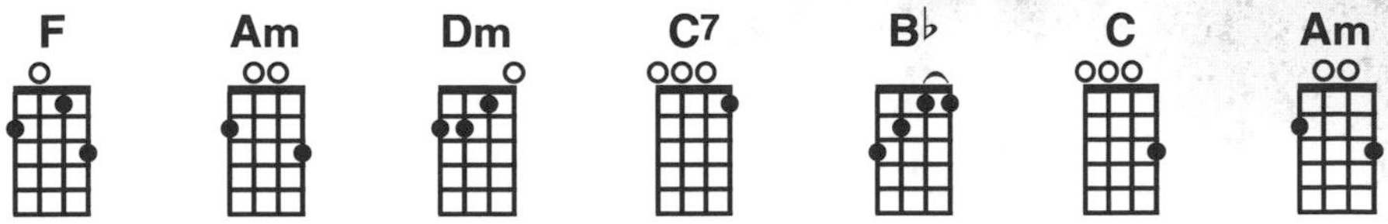

Intro	F	Am	Dm	C7	F	F

Verse 1

D
The guilty undertaker sighs
Am
The lonesome organ grinder cries
Dm   C7
The silver saxophones say I should refuse you
B♭
The cracked bells and washed-out horns
C
Blow into my face with scorn
Dm
But it's not that way
C7
I wasn't born to lose you

Chorus 1

F   Am
I want you, I want you
Dm   C7
I want you so bad
F
Honey, I want you

Verse 2

F
The drunken politician leaps
Am
Upon the street where mothers weep
Dm   C7
And the saviors who are fast asleep, they wait for you

cont.

B♭
And I wait for them to interrupt
C
Me drinkin' from my broken cup
Dm
And ask me to
C7
Open up the gate for you

Chorus 2

F Am
I want you, I want you
Dm C7
I want you so bad
F
Honey, I want you

Bridge

Am
How all my fathers, they've gone down
Dm
True love they've been without it
Am
But all their daughters put me down
B♭ C
'Cause I don't think about it

Verse 3

F
Well, I return to the Queen of Spades
Am
And talk with my chambermaid
Dm C7
She knows that I'm not afraid to look at her
B♭
She is good to me
C
And there's nothing she doesn't see
Dm
She knows where I'd like to be
C7
But it doesn't matter

Chorus 3

```
 F              Am
I want you, I want you
 Dm              C7
I   want you so bad
         F
Honey, I want you
```

Verse 4

```
          F
Now your dancing child with his Chinese suit
   Am
He spoke to me, I took his flute
Dm                               C7
No, I wasn't very cute to him,   was I?
     B♭
But I did it, though, because he lied
C
  And because he took you for a ride
Dm
  And because time was on his side
C7
  And because I…
```

Chorus 4

```
 F              Am
I want you, I want you
 Dm          C7
I want you so bad

Honey, I want (you)

| F        | Am       | Dm       | C7       |
  you
||: F      | Am       | Dm       | C7       :||  Repeat to fade
```

I PITY THE POOR IMMIGRANT

Words & Music by Bob Dylan

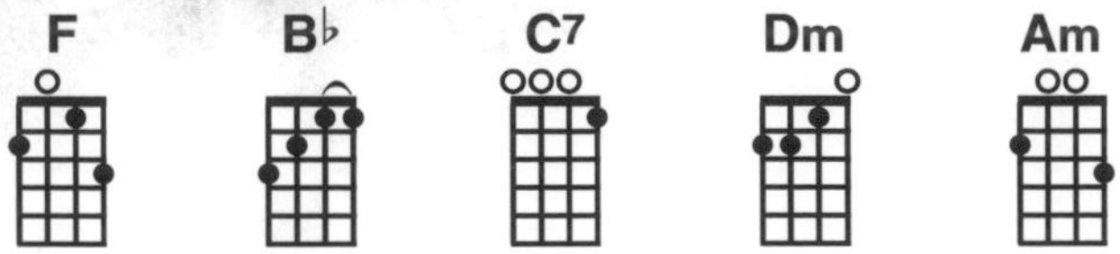

Intro ‖: F | B♭ | C7 | F :‖

Verse 1

```
F                B♭
I pity the poor immigrant
       C7                      F
Who wishes he would've stayed home
                                B♭
Who uses all his power to do evil
            C7                F
But in the end is always left so alone
      Dm                  Am
That man whom with his fingers cheats
            B♭          F
And who lies with ev'ry breath
                      B♭
Who passionately hates his life
      C7           F
And likewise, fears his death
```

Link 1 | F | B♭ | C7 | F ‖

Verse 2

F   B♭
I pity the poor immigrant
          C7   F
Whose strength is spent in vain
                              B♭
Whose heaven is like Ironsides
        C7   F
Whose tears are like rain
     Dm   Am
Who eats but is not satisfied
     B♭   F
Who hears but does not see
                                B♭
Who falls in love with wealth itself
     C7   F
And turns his back on me

Link 2 | F | B♭ | C7 | F ||

Verse 3

  F   B♭
I pity the poor immigrant
     C7   F
Who tramples through the mud
                                 B♭
Who fills his mouth with laughing
            C7   F
And who builds his town with blood
         Dm   Am
Whose visions in the final end
      B♭   F
Must shatter like glass
                   B♭
I pity the poor immigrant
             C7   F
When his gladness comes to pass

Outro

: F	B♭	C7	F :
Dm	Am	B♭	F
F	B♭	C7	F	

I SHALL BE RELEASED

Words & Music by Bob Dylan

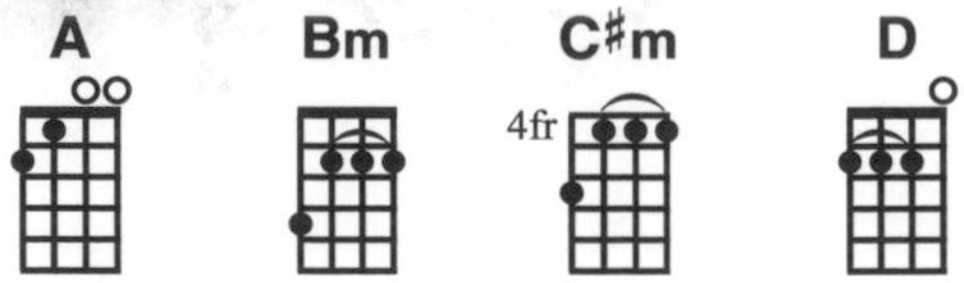

Intro | A | A | A ||

Verse 1

A   Bm
They say ev'rything can be replaced
C♯m   Bm   A   D
Yet ev'ry distance is not near
A   Bm
So I remember ev'ry face
C♯m   Bm   A   D
Of ev'ry man who put me here

Chorus 1

A   Bm
I see my light come shining
C♯m   Bm   A
From the west unto the east
                 Bm
Any day now, any day now
C♯m Bm   A
I shall be released

Verse 2

A   Bm
They say ev'ry man needs protection
C♯m   Bm   A   D
They say ev'ry man must fall
A   Bm
Yet I swear I see my reflection
C♯m   Bm   A   D
Some place so high above this wall

Chorus 2

```
A                         Bm
  I see my light come shining
C#m        Bm        A
  From the west unto the east
                Bm
Any day now,  any day now
C#m Bm       A
  I  shall be released
```

Verse 3

```
A                              Bm
  Standing next to me in this lonely crowd
C#m              Bm                A    D
  Is a man who swears he's not to blame
A                          Bm
  All day long I hear him shout so loud
C#m          Bm         A       D
  Crying out that he was framed
```

Chorus 3

```
A                         Bm
  I see my light come shining
C#m        Bm             A
  From the west unto the east
                Bm
Any day now,  any day now
C#m Bm       A
  I  shall be released
```

Outro

```
| A        | Bm       | C#m  Bm | A  D   A |
| A        | Bm       | C#m  Bm | A        ||
```

I THREW IT ALL AWAY

Words & Music by Bob Dylan

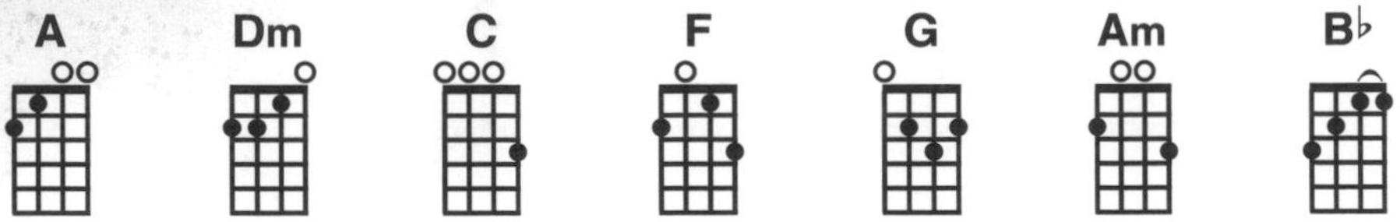

Intro | A Dm | C F | C G | C ‖

```
         C                 Am F      C
Verse 1    I once held her       in my arms
         C              Am             F      G
           She said she would always   stay
         A              Dm
           But I was cruel
           C               F   C
         I treated her like a fool
         F                  C     F
           I threw it all a - way

         C            Am         F                   C
Verse 2    Once I had mountains  in the palm of my hand
         C                 Am                  F      G
           And rivers that ran through ev'ry day
         A                  Dm
           I must have been mad
                 C          F   C
         I never knew what I had
               F            C     F
         Until I threw it all a - way
```

```
            F                  G     C                       Am
Chorus 1    Love is all there is, it makes the world go 'round
            F               G                          A
            Love and only love, it can't be den - ied
            F                         G
               No matter what you think about it
            C                              A
               You just won't be able to do without it
            B♭                              F       G
               Take a tip from one who's tried

            C                     Am     F                              C
Verse 3        So if you find someone who gives you all of her love
                                     Am          F      G
            Take it to your heart, don't let it stray
                A                 Dm
            For one thing that's certain
                       C             F
            You will surely be a-hurtin'
            C                   F       C      F
               If you throw it all a - way
            C                  G      C
               If you throw it all a - way

Outro       | A  Dm | C    F  | C  G  | C      ||
```

IDIOT WIND

Words & Music by Bob Dylan

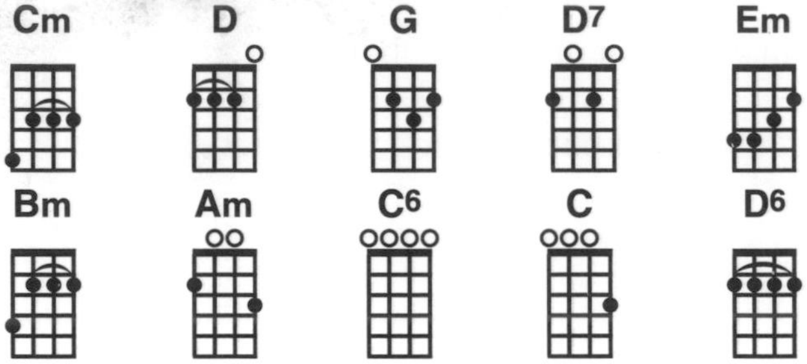

Verse 1

Cm **D** **G**
Someone's got it in for me, they're planting stories in the press
Cm
Whoever it is I wish they'd cut it out
D **D7** **G** **D**
But when they will I can only guess
Em **Bm** **Am** **G**
They say I shot a man named Gray and took his wife to Italy
Em **Bm** **Am** **G**
She inherited a million bucks and when she died it came to me
Bm **C6**
I can't help it if I'm lucky

Verse 2

Cm **D** **D7** **G**
People see me all the time and they just can't remember how to act
Cm **D** **D7** **G** **D**
Their minds are filled with big ideas, images and distorted facts
Em **Bm** **Am** **G** **D**
Even you, yesterday you had to ask me where it was at
Em **Bm** **Am** **G**
I couldn't believe after all these years, you didn't know me better than that
Bm **C6**
Sweet lady

Chorus 1

G **C** **G**
Idiot wind, blowing every time you move your mouth
C **D6** **D7**
Blowing down the backroads headin' south
G **C** **G**
Idiot wind, blowing every time you move your teeth

```
                  C
cont.     You're an idiot, babe

             D              D7                G       C  G  C
          It's a wonder that you still know how to breathe


            Cm                              D
Verse 3   I ran into the fortune-teller, who said beware of

          D7                   G
          Lightning that might strike

          Cm                               D
          I haven't known peace and quiet for so long

            D7                       G     D
          I can't remember what it's like

                    Em          Bm             Am                          G
          There's a lone soldier on the cross, smoke pourin' out of a boxcar door

          Em                          Bm
          You didn't know it, you didn't think it could be done,

          Am                  G
          In the final end he won the wars

                Bm            C6
          After losin' every battle


          Cm                           D
Verse 4   I woke up on the roadside, daydreamin' 'bout the

          D7                        G
          Way things sometimes are

          Cm                                      D
          Visions of your chestnut mare shoot through my head and are

          D7                G     D
          Makin' me see stars

          Em                         Bm               Am          G
          You hurt the ones that I love best and cover up the truth with lies

          Em                    Bm          Am               G
          One day you'll be in the ditch, flies buzzin' a - round your eyes

          Bm              C6
          Blood on your saddle


          G           C                                      G
Chorus 2  Idiot wind, blowing through the flowers on your tomb

          C                                        D6
          Blowing through the curtains in your room

          G           C                                    G
          Idiot wind, blowing every time you move your teeth

                            C
          You're an idiot, babe

             D              D7                G       C  G  C
          It's a wonder that you still know how to breathe
```

Verse 5

Cm D D7 G
It was gravity which pulled us down and destiny which broke us a - part

Cm D
You tamed the lion in my cage but it just

D7 G D
Wasn't e - nough to change my heart

Em Bm
Now everything's a little upside down,

Am G
As a matter of fact the wheels have stopped

Em Bm
What's good is bad, what's bad is good,

Am G
You'll find out when you reach the top

Bm C6
You're on the bottom

Verse 6

Cm D D7 G
I noticed at the ceremony, your cor - rupt ways had finally made you blind

Cm
I can't remember your face anymore,

D D7 G D
Your mouth has changed, your eyes don't look into mine

Em Bm
The priest wore black on the seventh day

Am G
And sat stone-faced while the building burned

Em Bm Am
I waited for you on the running boards, near the cypress trees,

G Bm C6
While the springtime turned slowly into Autumn

Chorus 3

G C G
Idiot wind, blowing like a circle around my skull

C D6 D7
From the Grand Coulee Dam to the Capi - tol

G C G
Idiot wind, blowing every time you move your teeth

C
You're an idiot, babe

D D7 G C G C
It's a wonder that you still know how to breathe

```
           Cm                              D            D7                          G
*Verse 7*  I can't feel you anymore, I can't even touch the books you've read
           Cm
           Every time I crawl past your door,
                 D                    D7                   G         D
           I been wishin' I was    somebody else instead
           Em                       Bm                  Am                  G
           Down the highway, down the tracks, down the road to ecstasy
             Em                     Bm                Am                G
           I followed you be - neath the stars, hounded by your memory
                Bm       C6
           And all your ragin' glory

           Cm                                              D
*Verse 8*  I been double-crossed now for the very last time
               D7                 G
           And now I'm finally free
             Cm                                                D
           I kissed goodbye the howling beast on the borderline
                  D7                         G    D
           Which separated you from me
           Em                          Bm                 Am              G
           You'll never know the hurt I suffered nor the pain I rise above
               Em                       Bm
           And I'll never know the same about you,
           Am                          G
           Your holiness or your kind of love
                  Bm                   C6
           And it makes me feel so sorry

            G              C                                     G
*Chorus 4*  Idiot wind, blowing through the buttons of our coats
            C                                      D6       D7
            Blowing through the letters that we wrote
            G              C                                    G
            Idiot wind, blowing through the dust upon our shelves
                           C
            We're idiots, babe
                  D                   D7                  G         C  G  C
            It's a wonder we can even feed our - selves

*Outro*     |: Cm      | D         | G        :|

            |: Em      | Bm        | Am        | G        :|

            | Bm C6    | C6  Cm    | Cm        ||
```

IF NOT FOR YOU

Words & Music by Bob Dylan

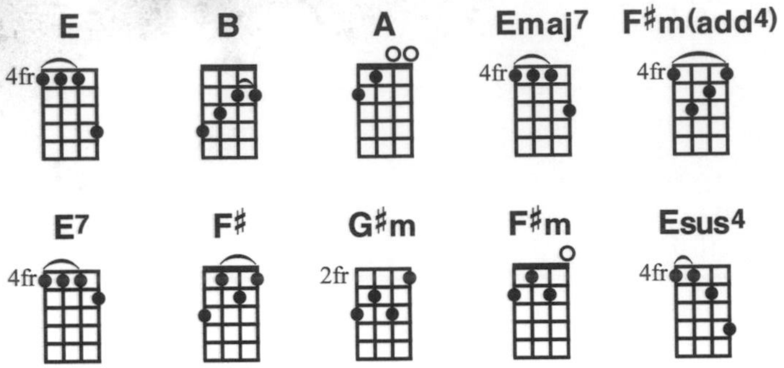

Intro

```
| E    B | A    B | E    B | A    B | E    B | A        |
| Emaj7 | F♯m(add4) | Emaj7 | F♯m(add4) | E  B | A    B | E    B ||
```

Verse 1

```
A           E    B
  If not for you
A                E              B
  Babe, I couldn't find the door
A               E
  Couldn't even see the floor
A                  Emaj7  F♯m(add4)
  I'd be sad and blue,      if not for you
```

Link 1

```
| E    B | A    B | E    B ||
```

Verse 2

```
A           E    B
  If not for you
A                E            B
  Babe, I'd lay awake all night
A              E
  Wait for the mornin' light
A               Emaj7
  To shine in through
F♯m(add4)                 Emaj7  F♯m(add4)
  But it would not be new,      if not for you
```

Link 2

```
| E    B | A    B | E    B | A        ||
```

Bridge 1

```
A
   If not for you
E
   My sky would fall
B                      E     E7
   Rain would gather too
A                                E
   Without your love I'd be nowhere at all
F♯                    B              A           G♯m    F♯m
I'd be lost if not for you, and you know it's true
```

Link 3

```
| B      A    | G♯m    F♯m  | B      A    | G♯m    F♯m  |
| B      A    | G♯m    F♯m  | E    Esus4  | E           ||
```

Bridge 2

```
A
   If not for you
E
   My sky would fall
B                      E     E7
   Rain would gather too
A                                E
   Without your love I'd be nowhere at all
F♯                   B    A        G♯m    F♯m
Oh! What would I do, if not for you
```

Link 4

```
| B      A    | G♯m    F♯m  | B      A    | G♯m    F♯m  |
| B      A    | G♯m    F♯m  | E    Esus4  | E           ||
```

Verse 3

```
                E     B
If not for you,
A               E              B
   Winter would have no spring
A                   E
   Couldn't hear the robin sing
A                            Emaj7
   I just wouldn't have a clue
F♯m(add4)                        Emaj7  F♯m(add4)      E   B
   Anyway it wouldn't ring true,          if not for you
```

Coda

```
||:  A                E   B
      If not for you          :||   Repeat to fade
```

IF YOU SEE HER, SAY HELLO

Words & Music by Bob Dylan

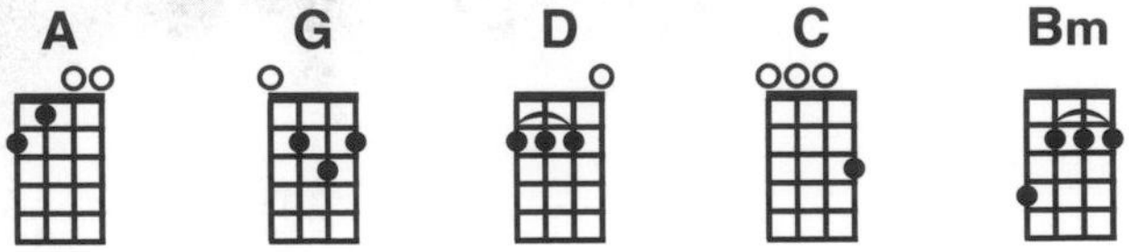

Intro

```
| A     | G     | A     | G    A |
| D     | D     | A     | G      |
| A     | G     | A     | G      |
| D     | D     ||
```

Verse 1

```
D                    G        D     A                    D
  If you see her, say hello,    she might be in Tangier
                        G            D                  C     A
She left here last early Spring, is livin' there, I hear___
Bm                   G      D                          G
   Say for me that I'm all right though things get kind of slow
            Bm                   D                  G              D
She might think that I've for - gotten her, don't tell her it isn't so
```

Verse 2

```
D          G          D          A             D
We had a falling - out, like lovers often will
                              G         D                            C     A
And to think of how she left that night, it still brings me a chill___
     Bm                  G    D                      G
And though our sepa - ration, it pierced me to the heart
Bm                    D                    G              D
   She still lives in - side of me, we've never been a - part
```

Verse 3

D   G   D A   D
   If you get close to her,   kiss her once for me
                          G   D   C   A
I always have re - spected her for busting out and gettin' free___
  Bm   G   D   G
Oh, whatever makes her happy,   I won't stand in the way
               Bm   D
Though the bitter taste still lingers on
            G   D
From the night I tried to make her stay

Verse 4

D   G   D A   D
I see a lot of people   as I make the rounds
                                G   D   C   A
And I hear her name here and there as I go from town to town___
              Bm   A   D   G
And I've never gotten used to it, I've just learned to turn it off
Bm   D   G   D
Either I'm too sensitive or else I'm gettin' soft

Verse 5

D   G   D   A   D
   Sundown, yellow moon, I replay the past
                   G   D   C   A
I know every scene by heart, they all went by so fast___
Bm   G   D   G
If she's passin' back this way, I'm not that hard to find
Bm   D   G   D
Tell her she can look me up if she's got the time

Outro

||: D | A | G | A |
| G | A | G | D :||

I'LL BE YOUR BABY TONIGHT

Words & Music by Bob Dylan

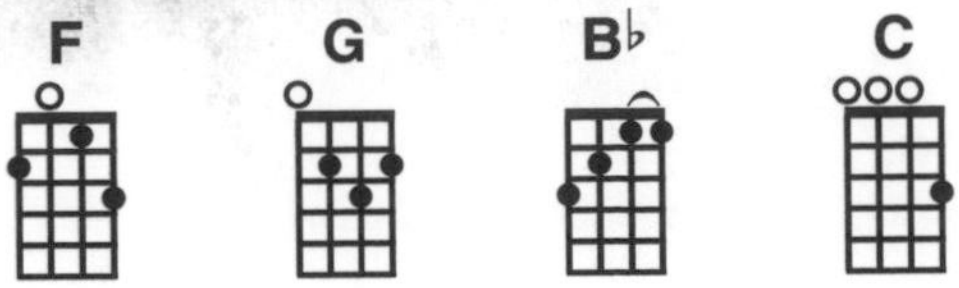

Intro | F | F | G | G |
| B♭ | C | F | F ||

Verse 1
F
Close your eyes,
Close the door
You don't have
G
To worry any more
B♭ C F C
I'll be your___ baby tonight

Verse 2
F
Shut the light,
Shut the shade
G
You don't have
To be afraid
B♭ C F
I'll be your___ baby tonight

Bridge
B♭
Well, that mockingbird's gonna sail away
F
We're gonna forget it

cont.

```
       G
That big, fat moon is gonna shine like a spoon
   C    N.C.
 But     we're gonna let it

You won't regret it
```

Verse 3

```
               F
Kick your shoes off,

Do not fear
               G
Bring that bottle

Over here
B♭               C          F
   I'll be your___ baby tonight
```

Outro

```
| F      | F      | G      | G      |
| B♭     | C      | F      | F      ||  To fade
```

I'LL KEEP IT WITH MINE

Words & Music by Bob Dylan

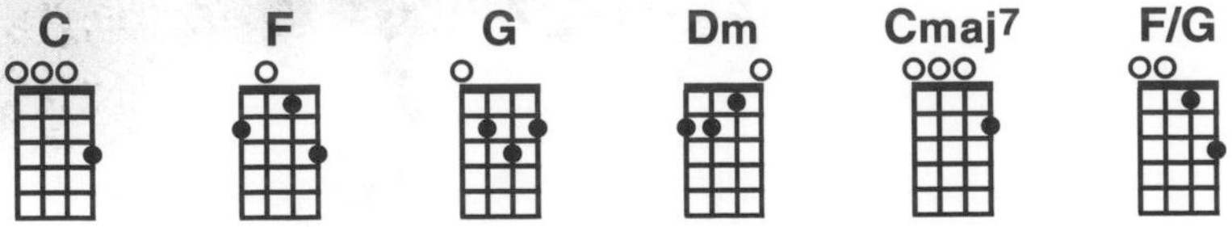

Intro | C | C | F | C F | C | C ||

Verse 1

(C) F C F C
You will search, babe
F C G F
At a - ny cost
C F C F
But how long, babe
C F C G C F
Can you search for what's not lost?
C F C F C F C
Ev - ery - body will help you
F C F
Some people are ve - ry kind
C F C Dm C F C G F
But if I can save you a - ny time
C Cmaj7 F C F
Come on, give it to me
C Dm F/G (C)
I'll keep it with mine

Link | C F C | F C G C | C F C |
| G | G ||

Verse 2

```
(G)    C     F  C
I can't help it
  F   C    F    G   F
If you might think I'm odd
   C   F       C    F  C   F              C
If I say I'm not lov - ing you for what you are
        G           F
But for what you're not
C    F   C    F   C    F    C
Eve - ry - body will help you
           F         C  F
Discover what you set out to find
       C    F    C         F     C  F C
But if I can save you any time
C       Cmaj7  F      C F
Come on,      give it to me
C   Dm     F/G  C     F
I'll keep it with mine
```

Harmonica break

| C   F   C | C | C | C ||

Verse 3

```
(C)                    F  C
The train leaves
   F    C    G  F C  F  C  Dm  C
At half past ten
F          C        F C
   But it'll be back     tomorrow
F     C  F    C    F
Same    time   a - gain
           C     F  C  F C   F      C
The con - ductor          he's weary
       F   C    F
He's still stuck on the line
      C F C     F     C   G    F
But if I        can save you any time
C          F       C F
Come on, give it to me
C   Dm     F/G  C     F    C
I'll keep it with mine
```

IS YOUR LOVE IN VAIN?

Words & Music by Bob Dylan

D A Bm G

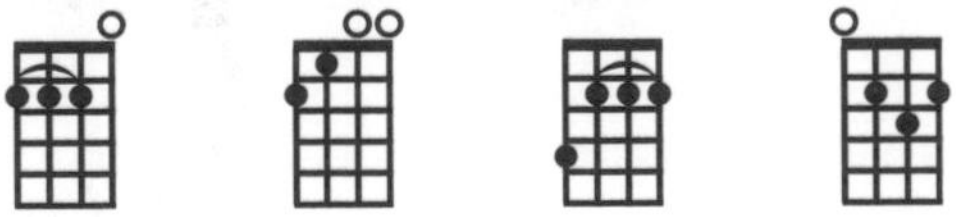

```
Intro    | D  | A  | Bm | D  | G  | A  | A  | A  |

         | D  | A  | Bm | D  | G  | G  | A  | A  |

         | Bm | A  | G  | D  | G  | G  | A  | A  |

         | D  | A  | Bm | D  | G  | A  | D  | D  |


                   D    A  Bm  D          G                  A
Verse 1  Do you love me,          or are you  just extending goodwill?
                   D      A       Bm         D         G              A
         Do you need me half as bad as you say, or are you just feeling guilt?
                   Bm       A      G        D
         I've been burned before and I know the score
                 G              A
         So you won't hear me complain
         D           A       Bm      D
            Will I be able to count on you
           F      A     D
         Or is your love in vain?


              D      A             Bm      D          G          A  D
Verse 2  Are you so fast that you cannot see that I must have solitude?
                       A   Bm           D  G            A
         When I am in the darkness,        why do you intrude?
                  Bm       A               G         D
         Do you know my world, do you know my kind
         G           A
         Or must I explain?
         D           A     Bm   A
            Will you let me be myself
           G      A     D
         Or is your love in vain?
```

Link

G A D A Bm
Well I've been to the mountain and I've been in the wind
G A D
I've been in and out of happiness
G A D A Bm
I have dined with kings, I've been offered wings
G A
And I've never been too impressed

Verse 3

D A Bm D G A D
All right, I'll take a chance, I will fall in love with you
A Bm D G A
If I'm a fool, you can have the night, you can have the morning too
Bm A G D
Can you cook and sew, make flowers grow
G A
Do you understand my pain?
D A Bm D
Are you willing to risk it all
G A D
Or is your love in vain?

Instrumental

| D | A | Bm | D | G | A | D | D |
| D | A | Bm | D | G | G | A | A ||

Outro

Bm A G D
Can you cook and sew, make flowers grow
G A
Do you understand my pain?
D A Bm D
Are you willing to risk it all
G A D
Or is your love in vain?

| D | A | Bm | D | G | A | D | D ||

ISIS

Words by Bob Dylan & Jacques Levy
Music by Bob Dylan

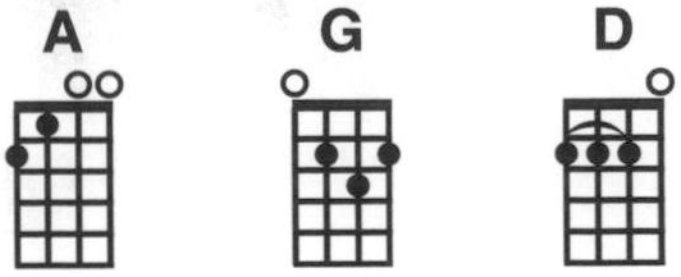

To match original recording, tune ukulele up a semitone

Intro | A | A | A | A ||

Verse 1
```
A          G            D            A
I married Isis on the fifth day of May
                           G       D          A
But I could not hold on to her very long
                      G           D            A
So I cut off my hair and I rode straight away
                            G                     D               A
For the wild unknown country where I could not go wrong
```

Verse 2
```
  A          G               D              A
I came to a high place of darkness and light
                      G                    D         A
The dividing line ran through the center of town
                    G           D           A
I hitched up my pony to a post on the right
               G             D                    A
Went into a laundry to wash my clothes down
```

Verse 3
```
   A          G          D                   A
A man in the corner approached me for a match
                      G          D          A
I knew right away   he was not ordinary
                      G                       D        A
He said, "Are you lookin' for somethin' easy to catch?"
                            G                    D        A
I said, "I got no money."  He said, "That ain't necessary"
```

Link 1 |: A G | D A :|

Verse 4

```
    A            G            C           A
We set out that night for the cold in the North
                G           D            A
I gave him my blanket, he gave me his word
                       G                      D              A
I said, "Where are we goin'?" He said we'd be back by the fourth
                   G                    D    A
I said, "That's the best news that I've ever heard"
```

Link 2

```
|: A   G | D   A :|
```

Verse 5

```
         A             G               D              A
I was thinkin' about turquoise, I was thinkin' about gold
                      G                  D               A
I was thinkin' about diamonds and the world's biggest necklace
                           G                     D       A
As we rode throught the canyons, through the devilish cold
                      G              D                A
I was thinkin' about Isis, how she thought I was so reckless
```

Verse 6

```
          A             G                  D         A
How she told me that one day we would meet up again
                       G            D             A
And things would be different the next time we wed
                 G            D          A
If I only could hang on and just be her friend
                        G      D              A
I still can't remember all the best things she said
```

Link 3

```
|: A   G | D   A :|
```

Verse 7

```
     A             G            D               A
We came to the pyramids all embedded in ice
                     G         D            A
He said, "There's a body I'm tryin' to find
             G       D                 A
If I carry it out it'll bring a good price"
                   G              D               A
'Twas then that I knew what he had on his mind
```

Verse 8

A G D A
The wind it was howlin' and the snow was outrageous

G D A
We chopped through the night and we chopped through the dawn

G D A
When he died I was hopin' that it wasn't contagious

G D A
But I made up my mind that I had to go on

Link 4

| A G | D A | A | A |

Verse 9

A G D A
I broke into the tomb, but the casket was empty

G D A
There was no jewels, no nothin', I felt I'd been had

G D A
When I saw that my partner was just bein' friendly

G D A
When I took up his offer I must-a been mad

Link 5

|: A G | D A :| *Play 4 times*

| A | A ||

Verse 10

A G D A
I picked up his body and I dragged him inside

G D A
Threw him down in the hole and I put back the cover

G D A
I said a quick prayer and I felt satisfied

G D A
Then I rode back to find Isis just to tell her I love her

Link 6

| A G | D A |

Verse 11

A G D A
She was there in the meadow where the creek used to rise

G D A
Blinded by sleep and in need of a bed

G D A
I came in from the East with the sun in my eyes

G D A
I cursed her one time then I rode on ahead

Link 7

```
||: A   G | D   A :||  Play 4 times
```

Verse 12

```
       A                   G                   D           A
She said, "Where ya been?" I said, "No place special"
                         G                D                 A
She said, "You look different." I said, "Well, not quite"
                         G        D                       A
She said, "You been gone." I said, "That's only natural"
                           G                              D  A
She said, "You gonna stay?" I said, "Yeah, I jes might"
```

Link 8

```
||: A   G | D   A :||  Play 4 times
```

Verse 13

```
A        G          D          A
Isis, oh, Isis, you mystical child
                        G              D              A
What drives me to you is what drives me insane
            G                  D              A
I still can remember the way that you smiled
                        G               D        A
On the fifth day of May in the drizzlin' rain
```

Outro

```
||: A   G | D   A :||  Play 4 times
```

IT AIN'T ME, BABE

Words & Music by Bob Dylan

G C D(add4) Bm Am D

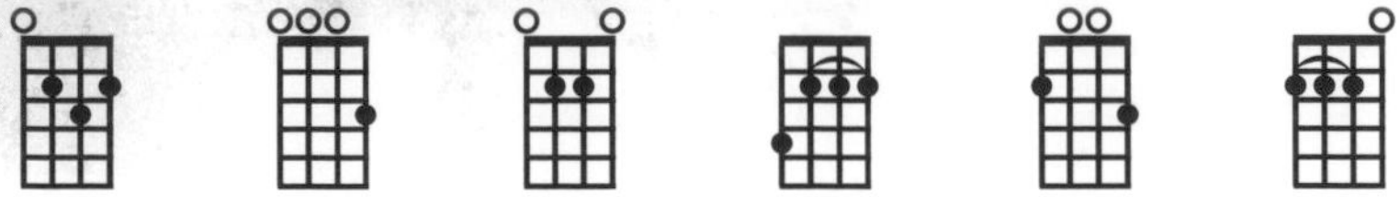

Intro | G | C | G | G ||

Verse 1

```
    Dadd4          C
Go 'way from my window
Dadd4                     G   C   G
Leave at your own chosen speed
   Dadd4             C
I'm not the one you want, babe
    Dadd4            G   C   G
I'm not the one you need
      Bm                Am
You say you're lookin' for someone
         Bm               Am
Never weak but always strong
            Bm               Am
To pro - tect you an' de - fend you
            Bm             Am
Whether you are right or wrong
          C                              D
Some - one to open each and every door
```

Chorus 1

```
              G
But it ain't me, babe
C         D         G
No, no, no, it ain't me, babe
          C           D       G
It ain't me you're lookin' for, babe
```

Link 1 | Dadd4 | C D | G C | G ||

Verse 2

```
     Dadd4            C
Go lightly from the ledge, babe
     Dadd4           G   C   G
Go lightly on the ground
```

cont.

Dadd4 C
I'm not the one you want, babe

Dadd4 G C G
I will only let you down

Bm Am
You say you're lookin' for someone

Bm Am
Who will promise never to part

Bm Am
Some - one to close his eyes for you

Bm Am
Some - one to close his heart

C D
Some - one who will die for you an' more

Chorus 2

As Chorus 1

Link 2

| Dadd4 | C | Dadd4 | G C | G ‖

Verse 3

Dadd4 C
Go melt back into the night, babe

Dadd4 G C G
Everything inside is made of stone

Dadd4 C
There's nothing in here moving

Dadd4 G C G
An' anyway I'm not alone

Bm Am
You say you're lookin' for someone

Bm Am
Who'll pick you up each time you fall

Bm Am
To gather flowers constantly

Bm Am
An' to come each time you call

C D
A lover for your life an' nothing more

Chorus 3

As Chorus 1

Outro

| Dadd4 | C | Dadd4 | G C | G ‖

IT'S ALL OVER NOW, BABY BLUE

Words & Music by Bob Dylan

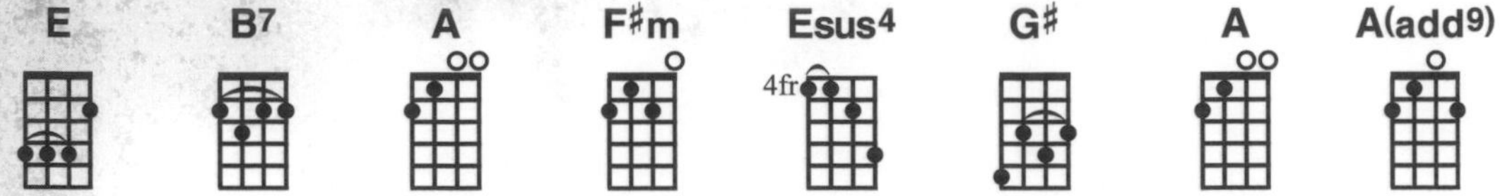

Intro | E | E | E | E ||

Verse 1

B7   A   E
You must leave now, take what you need, you think will last
          B7   A   E
But whatever you wish to keep, you better grab it fast
F♯m   A   E   Esus4 E
Yonder stands your orphan with his gun
F♯m   A   E   Esus4 E
Crying like a fire in the sun
G♯   A   B7
Look out the saints are comin' through
     F♯m   A(add9)   E
And it's all over now, Baby Blue

Verse 2

     B7   A   E
The highway is for gamblers, better use your sense
B7   A   E
Take what you have gathered from coincidence
     F♯m   A   E   Esus4 E
The empty-handed painter from your streets
   F♯m   A   E   Esus4 E
Is drawing crazy patterns on your sheets
G♯   A   B7
This sky, too, is folding under you
     F♯m   A(add9)   E
And it's all over now, Baby Blue

Verse 3

```
B7                              A        E
All your seasick sailors, they are rowing home
   B7                            A       E
All your reindeer armies, are all going home
   F♯m         A                         E     Esus4  E
The lover who just walked out your door
     F♯m             A                  E        Esus4  E
Has taken all his blankets from the floor
     G♯                           A            B7
The carpet, too, is moving under you
      F♯m          A(add9)     E
 And it's all over now, Baby Blue
```

Link

```
| B7   A    | E            | B7   A      | E          |
| F♯m  A    | E Esus4 E    | F♯m  A      | E          |
| G♯      A | B7           | F♯m A(add9) | E          ||
```

Verse 4

```
              B7                             A          E
Leave your stepping stones behind, something calls for you
   B7                                A        E
Forget the dead you've left, they will not follow you
     F♯m                A                  E       Esus4  E
The vagabond who's rapping at your door
   F♯m              A                        E        Esus4  E
Is standing in the clothes that you once wore
G♯                              A      B7
Strike another match, go start anew
      F♯m          A(add9)      E      Esus4  E
And it's all over now, Baby Blue
```

Coda

```
| B7        | E         ||
```

IT'S ALRIGHT, MA (I'M ONLY BLEEDING)

Words & Music by Bob Dylan

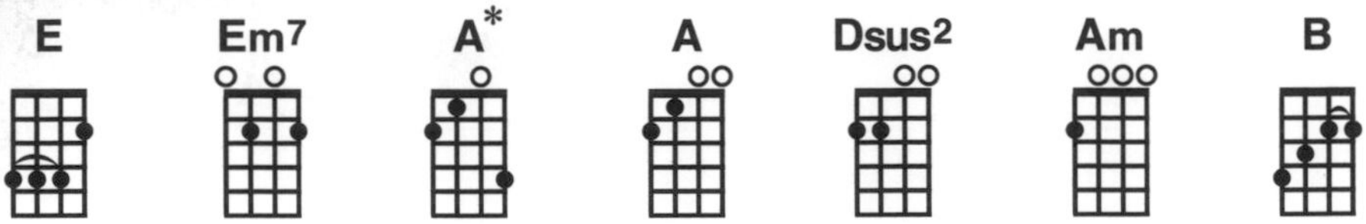

Intro | E | Em7 A* Em7 | E | Em7 A* Em7 |
| E | Em7 A* Em7 | E | E ||

Verse 1

```
A
Darkness at the break of noon
E
Shadows even the silver spoon
     Dsus2
The handmade blade, the child's balloon
  A
E - clipses both the sun and moon
   Am
To understand you know too soon
                   (E)
There is no sense in trying
```

Link 1 | E | Em7 A* Em7 | E | Em7 A* Em7 |
| E | Em7 A* Em7 | E | E ||

Verse 2

```
A
Pointed threats, they bluff with scorn
E
Suicide remarks are torn
            Dsus2
From the fool's gold mouthpiece the hollow horn
    A
Plays wasted words, proves to warn
     Am                          (E)
That he not busy being born is busy dying
```

Link 2 As Link 1

Verse 3

```
          A
Temp - tation's page flies out the door
     E
You follow, find yourself at war
         Dsus2
Watch waterfalls of pity roar
     A
You feel to moan but unlike before
              Am
You dis - cover that you'd just be one more
          (E)
Person crying
```

Link 3 | E | Em7 A* Em7 | E | Em7 A* Em7 | E | E ||

Chorus 1

```
E                   B
So don't fear if you hear
E                         A
  A foreign sound to your ear
E  B   A     B           E
It's al - right, Ma, I'm only sighing
```

Link 4 As Link 1

Verse 4

```
    A
As some warn victory, some downfall
E
Private reasons great or small
          Dsus2
Can be seen in the eyes of those that call
           A
To make all that should be killed to crawl
                 Am
While others say don't hate nothing at all
          (E)
Except hatred
```

Link 5 As Link 1

Verse 5

```
           A
Disil - lusioned words like bullets bark
   E
As human gods aim for their mark
         Dsus2
Make everything from toy guns that spark
   A
To flesh-colored Christs that glow in the dark
  Am
   It's easy to see without looking too far
                           (D)
That not much is really sacred
```

Link 6 As Link 3

Verse 6

```
         A
While preachers preach of evil fates
D
Teachers teach that knowledge waits
      Dsus2
Can lead to hundred-dollar plates
A
Goodness hides behind its gates
       Am
But even the president of the United States
                                (E)
Sometimes must have to stand naked
```

Link 7 As Link 1

Chorus 2

```
E                                         B
An' though the rules of the road have been lodged
                  E                 A
It's only people's games that you got to dodge
      E  B  A    B       E
And it's al - right, Ma, I can make it
```

Link 8 As Link 3

Verse 7

```
A
Advertising signs they con
E
You into thinking you're the one
           Dsus2
That can do what's never been done
           A
That can win what's never been won
Gm/B♭
Meantime life outside goes on
        (E)
All a - round you
```

Link 9 As Link 3

Verse 8

```
      A
You lose yourself, you reappear
      E
You suddenly find you got nothing to fear
    Dsus2
A - lone you stand with nobody near
          A
When a trembling distant voice, unclear
  Am
Startles your sleeping ears to hear
                                    (E)
That somebody thinks they really found you
```

Link 10 As Link 1

Verse 9

```
   A
A question in your nerves is lit
          E
Yet you know there is no answer fit
   Dsus2
To satisfy, insure you not to quit
             A
To keep it in your mind and not forget
              Am
That it is not he or she or them or it
                (E)
That you be - long to
```

Link 11 As Link 1

Chorus 3

```
E                                           B
Although the masters make the rules
          E                        A
For the wise men and the fools
E B   A          B            E
I  got nothing, Ma, to live up to
```

Link 12 As Link 1

Verse 10

```
              A
For them that must obey authority
               E
That they do not respect in any degree
               Dsus2
Who des - pise their jobs, their destinies
A
Speak jealously of them that are free
Am
   Cultivate their flowers to be
                                                     (E)
Nothing more than something they in - vest in
```

Link 13 As Link 1

Verse 11

```
          A
While some on principles baptized
E
To strict party platform ties
Csus2
Social clubs in drag disguise
A
Outsiders they can freely criticize
      Am
Tell nothing except who to idolize
                         (E)
And then say God bless him
```

Link 14 As Link 1

Verse 12

```
                A
While one who sings with his tongue on fire
E
Gargles in the rat race choir
Dsus2
Bent out of shape from society's pliers
A
   Cares not to come up any higher
       Am
But rather get you down in the hole
     (E)
That he's in
```

Link 15 As Link 1

Chorus 4

```
E                                B
But I mean no harm nor put fault
    E                         A
On anyone that lives in a vault
     E   B   A    B              E
But it's al - right, Ma, if I can't please him
```

Link 16 As Link 3

Verse 13

```
    A
Old lady judges watch people in pairs
E
Limited in sex, they dare
         Dsus2
To push fake morals, insult and stare
      A
While money doesn't talk, it swears
      Am
Ob - scenity, who really cares
                   (E)
Propaganda, all is phony
```

Link 17 As Link 1

Verse 14

```
      A
While them that defend what they cannot see
       E
With a killer's pride, security
  Dsus2
It blows the minds most bitterly
    A
For them that think death's honesty
         Am
Won't fall upon them naturally
                        (E)
Life sometimes must get lonely
```

Link 18 As Link 3

Verse 15

```
   E
My eyes collide head-on with stuffed
A
Graveyards, false gods, I scuff
   E
At pettiness which plays so rough
          Dsus2
Walk up - side-down inside handcuffs
A
Kick my legs to crash it off
        Am                                         (E)
Say o - kay, I have had enough, what else can you show me?
```

Link 19 As Link 3

Chorus 5

```
E                                  B
And if my thought-dreams could be seen
                 E                A
They'd probably put my head in a guillotine
    E  B   A   B                   E
But it's al  -  right, Ma, it's life, and life only
```

JOHN WESLEY HARDING

Words & Music by Bob Dylan

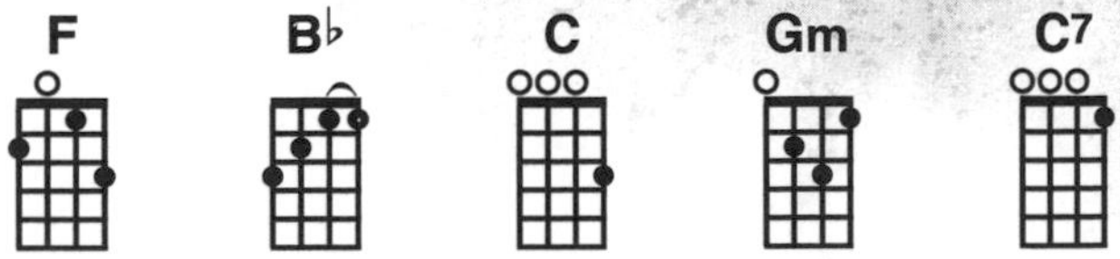

Intro | F | F ||

Verse 1

F B♭ C F
John Wesley Harding was a friend to the poor
Gm B♭ C
He trav'led with a gun in ev'ry hand
F B♭ C F
All along this countryside, he opened many a door
B♭ C7 F
But he was never known to hurt an honest man

Link 1

| F | F | B♭ C | F | F | F | Gm | B♭ C |
| F | F | B♭ C | F | F | B♭C | F | F ||

Verse 2

F B♭ C F
'Twas down in Chaynee County, a time they talk about
Gm B♭ C
With his lady by his side he took a stand
F B♭ C F
And soon the situation there was all but straightened out
B♭ C7 F
For he was always know to lend a helping hand

Link 2 As Link 1

Verse 3

F B♭ C F
All across the telegraph his name it did resound
Gm B♭ C
But no charge held against him could they prove
F B♭ C F
And there was no man around who could track or chain him down
B♭ C7 F
He was never known to make a foolish move

Outro As Link 1

JOKERMAN

Words & Music by Bob Dylan

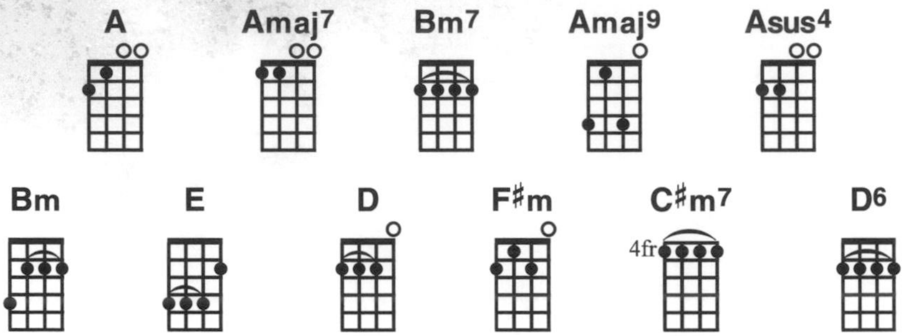

To match original recording, tune ukulele up a semitone

Verse 1

A Amaj7
Standing on the waters casting your bread
Bm7
While the eyes of the idol
Amaj9 A D/A
With the iron head are glowing
A Amaj7
Distant ships sailing into the mist
Bm7 Amaj9
You were born with a snake in both of your fists
A
While a hurricane was blowing
Bm E A
Freedom just around the corner for you
Bm E A D
But with truth so far off, what good will it do?

Chorus 1

E D
Jokerman dance to the nightingale tune
A E F♯m D
Bird fly high by the light of the moon
C♯m7 D6 E A
Oh, oh, oh, Jokerman

Verse 2

```
A                         Amaj7
   So swiftly the sun sets in the sky
Bm7                  Amaj9                      A     Asus4
   You rise up and say goodbye to no one
A                           Amaj7
   Fools rush in where angels fear to tread
Bm7                            Amaj9                    A
Both of their futures, so full of dread, you don't show one
Bm                  E                   A
   Shedding off one more layer of skin
           Bm                E                       A      D
Keeping one step ahead of the persecutor within
```

Chorus 2

```
E                             D
Jokerman dance to the nightingale tune
A          E             F#m          D
Bird fly high by the light of the moon
C#m7 D6  E   A
Oh,     oh,  oh, Jokerman
```

Verse 3

```
           A                                     Amaj7
You're a man of the mountains, you can walk on the clouds
          Bm7                            Amaj9           A      Asus4
Manipulator of crowds, you're a dream twister
                    A
You're going to Sodom and Gomorrah
     Amaj7
But what do you care?
       Bm7                      Amaj9                A
Ain't nobody there would want to marry your sister
Bm                            E                      A
Friend to the martyr, a friend to the woman of shame
                Bm
You look into the fiery furnace,
E                                    A       D
See the rich man without any name
```

Chorus 3

```
E                             D
Jokerman dance to the nightingale tune
A          E             F#m          D
Bird fly high by the light of the moon
C#m7 D6  E   A
Oh,    oh,  oh,  Jokerman
```

Link 1

```
| A       | Amaj7 | Bm7   | Amaj9 | A       | Asus4 ||
```

Verse 4

A Amaj7
Well, the Book of Leviticus and Deuteronomy
Bm7 Amaj9 A Asus4
The law of the jungle and the sea are your only teachers
A Amaj7
In the smoke of the twilight on a milk-white steed
Bm7 Amaj9 A
Michelangelo indeed could've carved out your features
Bm E A
Resting in the fields, far from the turbulent space
Bm E A D
Half asleep near the stars with a small dog licking your face

Chorus 4

E D
Jokerman dance to the nightingale tune
A E F♯m D
Bird fly high by the light of the moon
C♯m7 D6 E A
Oh, oh, oh, Jokermann

Link 2

| A | Amaj7 | Bm7 | Amaj9 | A | Asus4 ||

Verse 5

A Amaj7
Well, the rifleman's stalking the sick and the lame
Bm7 Amaj9 A Asus4
Preacherman seeks the same, who'll get there first is uncertain
A Amaj7
Nightsticks and water cannons, tear gas, padlocks
Bm7 Amaj9 A
Molotov cocktails and rocks behind every curtain
Bm E A
False-hearted judges dying in the webs that they spin
Bm E A D
Only a matter of time 'til night comes steppin' in

Chorus 5

E D
Jokerman dance to the nightingale tune
A E F♯m D
Bird fly high by the light of the moon
C♯m7 D6 E A
Oh, oh, oh, Jokerman

Link 3

| A | Amaj7 | Bm7 | Amaj9 | A | Asus4 ||

Verse 6

A   Amaj7
It's a shadowy world, skies are slippery gray

Bm7   Amaj9
A woman just gave birth to a prince today

A   Asus4
And dressed him in scarlet

A   Amaj7
He'll put the priest in his pocket, put the blade to the heat

Bm7   Amaj9
Take the motherless children off the street

A
And place them at the feet of a harlot

Bm   E   A
Oh, Jokerman, you know what he wants

Bm   E   A   D
Oh, Jokerman, you don't show any response

Chorus 6

E   D
Jokerman dance to the nightingale tune

A   E   F#m   D
Bird fly high by the light of the moon

C#m7 D6   E   A
Oh,   oh, oh, Jokerman

Coda

|: A | Amaj7 | Bm7 | Amaj9 | A | Asus4 :|

| Bm | E | A | A |

| Bm | E | A | D |

| E | D | A E | F#m ||

Fade out

JUST LIKE A WOMAN

Words & Music by Bob Dylan

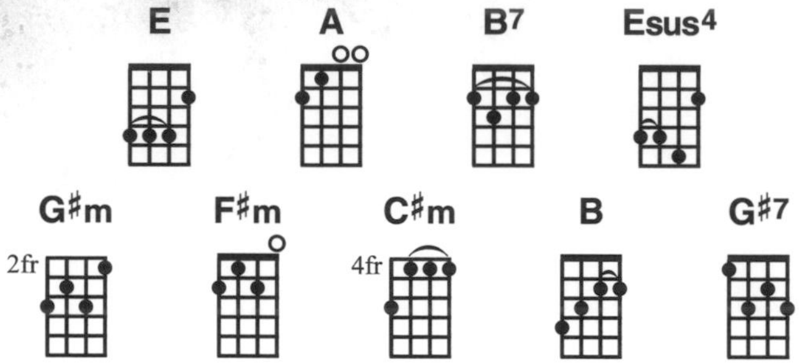

Intro | E A B7 | E | E A B7 | E |

Verse 1

E A B7 E Esus4 E
Nobody feels any pain
A B7 E Esus4 E
Tonight as I stand inside the rain
A B7
Ev'rybody knows
A B7
That Baby's got new clothes
A G♯m F♯m E B7
But late - ly I see her ribbons and her bows
C♯m E A B7
Have fallen from her curls

Chorus 1

E G♯m F♯m E A
She takes just like a woman, yes, she does
E G♯m F♯m E A
She makes love just like a woman, yes, she does
E G♯m F♯m E A
And she aches just like a woman
B7 E
But she breaks just like a little girl

Link 1 | A E A B | E ||

```
Verse 2        E     A    B7  E      Esus4   E
          Queen Mary, she's my friend
                         A        B7   E      Esus4   E
          Yes, I believe I'll go see her again
            A           B7
          Nobody has to guess
              A              B7
          That Baby can't be blessed
              A   G#m   F#m  E    B7
          Till she sees finally that she's like all the rest
                      C#m7            E     A        B7
          With her fog, her amphetamine   and her pearls
```

Chorus 2 As Chorus 1

```
Link 2    | A   E   A   B   | E          ||
```

```
                   G#7
Bridge    It was raining from the first

          And I was dying there of thirst
                 E
          So I    came in here
                      G#7
          And your    long-time curse hurts

          But what's worse
                   A
          Is this pain in here
          B7
             I can't stay in here

          Ain't it clear that –
```

Verse 3

```
E   A   B7  E       Esus4    E
I   just can't fit
                        A        B7  E     Esus4     E
Yes, I believe it's time for us to quit
A                 B7
When we meet again
A               B7
Introduced as friends
A       G#m  F#m E  B7
Please don't let  on that you knew me when
      C#m                  G#m  A B7
I was hungry and it was your      world
```

Chorus 3

```
          E    G#m  F#m  E  A
Ah, you fake just   like  a  woman, yes, you do
    E             G#m  F#m  E  A
You make love just  like  a  woman, yes, you do
           E    G#m  F#m  E  A
Then you ache just  like  a  woman

But you break just like a little girl
```

Link 3

```
| A  E  A  B  | E          ||
```

Coda

```
| E     A   B7 | E Esus4 E | E     A   B7 | E Esus4 E |
| A     B7     | A   B7    | A G#m F#m E  | B7        |
| C#m  E  A    | B7        | E G#m F#m E  | A         |
| E G#m F#m E  | A         | E G#m F#m E  | A         |
| B7           | A E A B   | E            ||
```

JUST LIKE TOM THUMB'S BLUES

Words & Music by Bob Dylan

Dsus2 D D/C C G D7

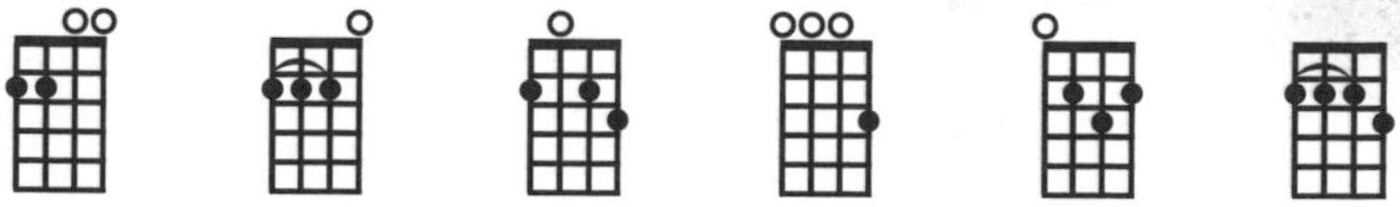

Intro 𝄆 Dsus2 D | D/C C | C G | C G 𝄇

Verse 1

G C
When you're lost in the rain in Juarez
D/C C G C G
When it's Eastertime too

And your gravity fails
C D/C C G C G
And negativity don't pull you through
C
Don't put on any airs
G
When you're down on Rue Morgue Avenue
D7
They got some hungry women there
G C G
And they really make a mess outta you

Verse 2

G
Now if you see Saint Annie
C D/C C G C G
Please tell her thanks a lot

I cannot move
C D/C C G C G
My fingers are all in a knot
C
I don't have the strength
G
To get up and take another shot

cont.

D7
And my best friend, my doctor
G C G
Won't even say what it is I've got

Verse 3

G
Sweet Melinda
C G C G
The peasants call her the goddess of gloom

She speaks good English
C D/C C G C G
And she invites you up into her room
C
And you're so kind
G C G
And careful not to go to her too soon
D7
And she takes your voice
G C G
And leaves you howling at the moon

Verse 4

G
Up on Housing Project Hill
C G
It's either fortune or fame

You must pick up one or the other
C D/C C G C G
Though neither of them are to be what they claim
C
If you're lookin' to get silly
G C G
You better go back to from where you came
D7
Because the cops don't need you
G C G
And man they expect the same

Verse 5

G
Now all the authorities
C D/C C G C G
They just stand around and boast
C
How they blackmailed the sergeant-at-arms
D/C C G C G
Into leaving his post

cont.

```
         C
And picking up Angel who
                                G      C  G
Just arrived here from the coast
             D7
Who looked so fine at first
                                 G      C  G
But left looking just like a  ghost
```

Solo

```
|: G        | C   D/C  C | G    C   | G      :|
|  C        | C          | G    C   | C       |
|  D7       | D7         | G    C   | G      ||
```

Verse 6

```
  G
I started out on burgundy
    C          D/C   C   G     C  G
But soon hit the hard - er  stuff
                              C
Everybody said they'd stand behind me
              D/C  C  G      C  G
When the game got rough
         C
But the joke was on me
                                            G     C  G
There was nobody even there to call my bluff
             D7
I'm going back to New York City
                          G       C  G
I do believe I've had enough
```

Coda

```
|: Dsus2  D | D/C  C | G    C | G     :|
```
Repeat to fade

KNOCKIN' ON HEAVEN'S DOOR

Words & Music by Bob Dylan

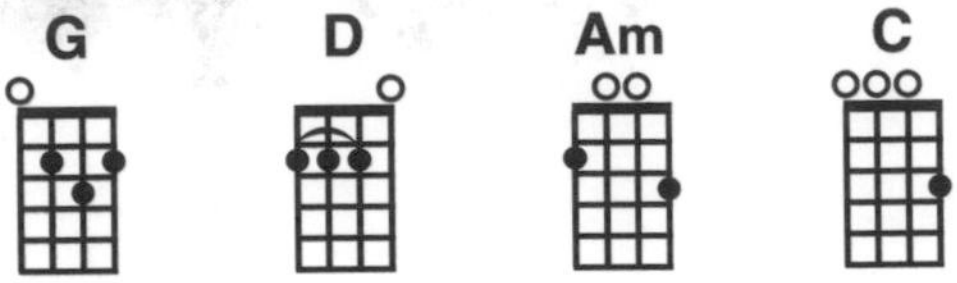

Intro ‖: G D | Am | G D | C :‖

Verse 1

G D Am
Mama, take this badge off of me
G D C
I can't use it anymore
G D Am
It's gettin' dark, too dark for me to see
G D C
I feel like I'm knockin' on heaven's door

Chorus 1

G D Am
Knock, knock, knockin' on heaven's door
G D C
Knock, knock, knockin' on heaven's door
G D Am
Knock, knock, knockin' on heaven's door
G D C
Knock, knock, knockin' on heaven's door

Verse 2

```
G                 D              Am
  Mama, put my guns in the ground
G            D              C
  I can't shoot them anymore
G                  D                   Am
  That long black cloud is comin' down
G                   D                      C
  I feel like I'm knockin' on heaven's door
```

Chorus 2

```
G                  D                     Am
  Knock, knock, knockin' on heaven's door
G                  D                     C
  Knock, knock, knockin' on heaven's  door
G                  D                     Am
  Knock, knock, knockin' on heaven's door
G                  D                     C
  Knock, knock, knockin' on heaven's door
```

Coda | G D | Am | G D | C || *Fade out*

LAY DOWN YOUR WEARY TUNE

Words & Music by Bob Dylan

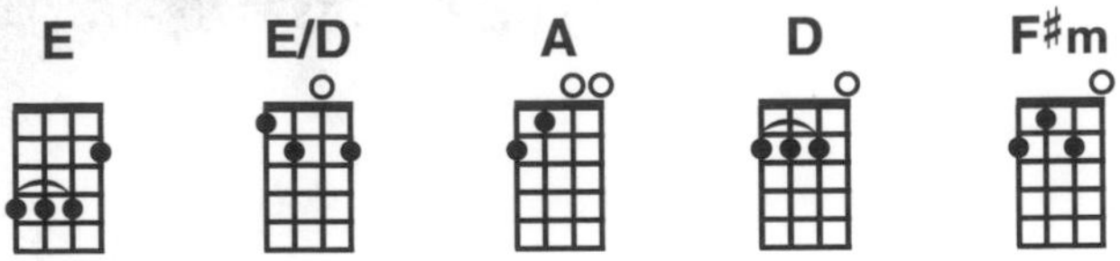

Chorus 1

```
E    E/D  A              D         A
Lay down your weary tune, lay down
                  F♯m       E
Lay down the song you strum
     E/D A                                D
And rest  yourself 'neath the strength of strings
                  A     E  E/D A
No voice can hope___ to____ hum
```

Verse 1

```
E           E/D  A                D            A
    Struck by    the sounds be - fore the sun
              F♯m       E
I knew the night had gone
    E/D      A                          D
The morn - ing breeze like a bugle blew
                 A      E  E/D A
Against the drums___ of____ dawn
```

Chorus 2 As Chorus 1

Verse 2

```
E    E/D A                   D        A
The o  -  cean wild like an organ played
                   F♯m     E
The seaweed's wove its strands
     E/D      A          E   A          D
The crash - in' waves like cymbals clashed
                 A      E E/D A
Against the rocks___    and  sands
```

Chorus 3 As Chorus 1

Verse 3

```
E   E/D  A                 D                 A
   I stood unwound be - neath the skies
                  F#m        E
And clouds un - bound by laws
    E/D  A        E       A        D
The cry - in' rain like a trumpet sang
                  A    E  E/D A
And asked for no___ ap  -  plause
```

Chorus 4 As Chorus 1

Verse 4

```
E      E/D A                 D          A
   The last  of leaves fell from the trees
                F#m          E
And clung to a new love's breast
    E/D    A                          D
The bran - ches bare like a banjo played
                    A     E     E/D A
To the winds that lis - tened____   best
```

Verse 5

```
E   E/D   A               D       A
   I gazed down in the river's mirror
                    F#m       E
And watched its winding strum
    E/D A                         D
The wa - ter smooth ran like a hymn
              A      E  E/D A
And like a harp___ did__  hum
```

Chorus 5 As Chorus 1

LAY, LADY, LAY

Words & Music by Bob Dylan

Intro ‖: A C♯m | G Bm :‖

Chorus 1

```
A              C♯m G          Bm               A     C♯m G Bm
   Lay, lady, lay,    lay across my big brass bed
A              C♯m G          Bm               A     C♯m G Bm
   Lay, lady, lay,    lay across my big brass bed
```

Verse 1

```
E              F♯m            A
   Whatever colors you have in your mind
E                     F♯m  A
   I'll show them to you and you'll see them shine
```

Chorus 2

```
A              C♯m G          Bm               A     C♯m G Bm
   Lay, lady, lay,    lay across my big brass bed
A                C♯m G                 Bm              A C♯m G Bm
   Stay, lady, stay,    stay with your man awhile
A                          C♯m   G                Bm                A C♯m G Bm
   Until the break of day,    let me see you make him smile
```

Verse 2

```
E                      F♯m        A
   His clothes are dirty but his hands are clean
E                      F♯m                A
   And you're the best thing that he's ever seen
```

Chorus 3

```
A                C♯m G                 Bm              A C♯m G Bm
   Stay, lady, stay,    stay with your man awhile
```

Bridge

```
C#m                                   E    D    A
   Why wait any longer for the world to begin
C#m                                   Bm       A
   You can have your cake and eat it too
C#m                                   E   D   A
   Why wait any longer for the one you love
              C#m                    Bm
When he's standing in front of you
```

Chorus 4

```
A            C#m G          Bm                      A C#m G Bm
   Lay, lady, lay,    lay across my big brass bed
A             C#m G                   Bm            A      C#m G Bm
   Stay, lady, stay,    stay while the night is still ahead
```

Verse 3

```
E            F#m          A
   I long to see you in the morning light
E            F#m         A
   I long to reach for you in the night
```

Chorus 5

```
A             C#m G                   Bm            A      C#m G Bm
   Stay, lady, stay,    stay while the night is still ahead
```

Coda

```
| A  Bm  | C#m  D | A        ||
```

LIFE IS HARD

Music by Bob Dylan
Words by Bob Dylan & Robert Hunter

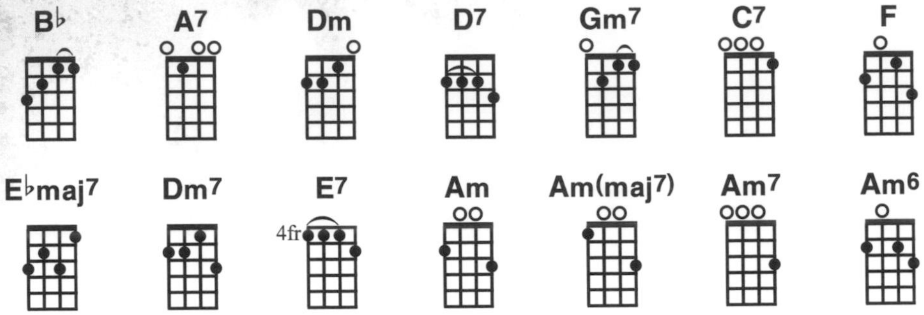

Intro

| B♭ | A7 | Dm | D7 |
| Gm7 | C7 | F | F ||

Verse 1

E♭maj7
The evening winds are still
Dm7 E7
I've lost the way and will
Am D7
Can't tell you where they went
Gm7 C7
I just know what they meant
Am Am(maj7)
I'm always on my guard
Am7 Am6
Admitting life is hard
Gm7 C7 F
With - out you near me

Verse 2

```
E♭maj7
   The friend you used to be
Dm7             E7
   So near and dear to me
Am                   D7
   You slipped so far away
Gm7               C7
   Where did we go a-stray
Am            Am(maj7)
   I pass the old schoolyard
Am7           Am6
   Admitting life is hard
Gm7     C7      F
   With - out you near me
```

Bridge

```
B♭                 A7
   Ever since the day
     Dm                    D7
The day you went away
Gm7               C7      F
I felt that empti - ness so wide
B♭                        A7
   I don't know what's wrong or right
  Dm               D7
I just know I need strength to fight
Gm7              C7        F              Am7
   Strength to fight that   world out - side
```

Verse 3

```
E♭maj7
   Since we've been out of touch
Dm7          E7
   I haven't felt that much
Am              D7
   From day to barren day
Gm7                 C7
   My heart stays locked away
Am            Am(maj7)
   I walk the boulevard
Am7           Am6
   Admitting life is hard
Gm7     C7      F
   With - out you near me
```

Verse 4

E♭maj7
The sun is sinking low

Dm7 E7
I guess it's time to go

Am D7
I feel a chilly breeze

Gm7 C7
In place of memories

Am Am(maj7)
My dreams are locked and barred

Am7 Am6
Admitting life is hard

Gm7 C7 F D7
With - out you near me

Outro

| B♭ | A7 | Dm | D7 |

Gm7 C7 F
With - out you near me

LIKE A ROLLING STONE

Words and Music by Bob Dylan

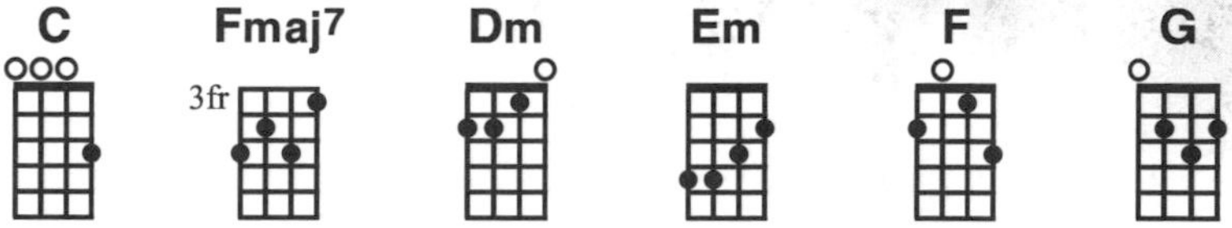


```
Intro      | C   Fmaj7 | C   Fmaj7 | C   Fmaj7 | C   Fmaj7 ||
```

```
           C                      Dm
Verse 1    Once upon a time you dressed so fine
                Em                          F              G
           You threw the bums a dime in your prime,   didn't you?
           C               Dm                       Em
           People'd call, say, "Beware doll, you're bound to fall"
                           F              G
           You thought they were all   kiddin' you
           F               G
             You used to   laugh about
           F                        G
             Everybody that was   hangin' out
           F             Em    Dm          C
             Now you don't talk so loud
           F             Em    Dm             C
             Now you don't seem so proud
             Dm                              F          G
           About having to be scrounging   for your next meal
```

```
                            C     F   G
Chorus 1   How does it feel
                            C     F   G
           How does it feel
                                C     F   G
           To be without a home
                                     C     F   G
           Like a complete unknown
                                 C     F   G
           Like a rolling stone?
```

```
Link 1     | C   F   | G         | G         ||
```

Verse 2

```
       C              Dm         Em
You've gone to the finest school all right, Miss Lonely
        F                         G
But you know you only used to get juiced in it
      C                        Dm                 Em
And nobody has ever taught you how to live on the street
                            F                 G
And now you find out you're gonna have to get used to it
F                      G
  You said you'd never compromise
F                                     G
  With the mystery tramp, but now you realize
F            Em        Dm C
  He's not selling any alibis
F                     Em     Dm     C
As you stare into the vacuum of his eyes
    Dm                    F     G
And ask him do you want to make a deal?
```

Chorus 2

```
             C   F   G
How does it feel
             C   F   G
How does it feel
              C   F   G
To be on your own
                   C   F   G
With no direction home
                    C   F   G
Like a complete unknown
                C   F   G
Like a rolling stone?
```

Link 2

```
| C   F  | G       | G       ||
```

Verse 3

```
    C            Dm
You never turned around to see the frowns
Em                     F
   On the jugglers and the clowns
                                G
When they all come down and did tricks for you
    C                        Dm
You never understood that it ain't no good
    Em                  F               G
You shouldn't let other people get your kicks for you
```

```
              F                                                      G
*cont.*          You used to ride on the chrome horse with your   diplomat
              F                                    G
                 Who carried on his shoulder a   Siamese cat
              F                Em               Dm          C
                 Ain't it hard   when you discover that
              F              Em     Dm          C
                 He really wasn't where it's at
              Dm                                       F          G
              After he took from you everything     he could steal
```

Chorus 3 As Chorus 2

```
Link 3        | C   F   | G         | G         ||
```

```
              C                    Dm                    Em
Verse 4          Princess on the steeple and all the   pretty people
                           F                           G
              They're all drinkin', thinkin' that they   got it made
              C                  Dm
                 Exchanging all    kinds of precious gifts and things
              Em                      F                        G
                 But you'd better lift your diamond ring,  you'd better pawn it babe
              F                  G
                 You used to be   so amused
              F                        G
                 At Napoleon in rags   and the language that he used
              F                      Em                     Dm       C
cont.            Go to him now, he calls you, you can't refuse
              F                   Em               Dm            C
                 When you got nothing, you got   nothing to lose
              Dm                                               F         G
                 You're invisible now, you got no secrets     to conceal
```

Chorus 4 As Chorus 2

```
Coda          |: C   F   | G         | C   F   | G         :|  Repeat to fade
```

LOVE MINUS ZERO/NO LIMIT

Words & Music by Bob Dylan

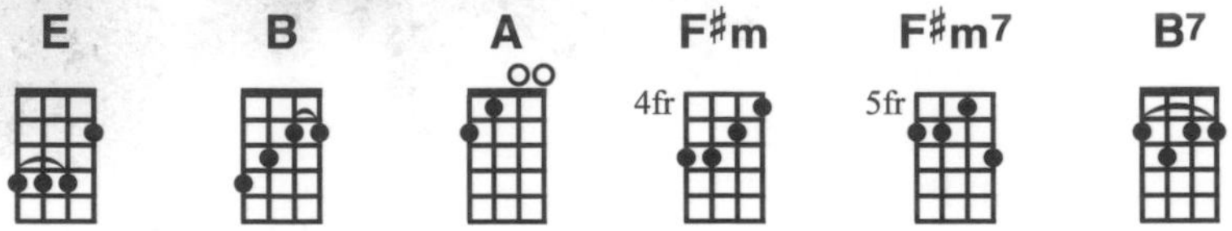

Intro | E | E ||

Verse 1

E
My love she speaks like silence
B A E
Without ideals or violence
B A E
She doesn't have to say she's faithful
F♯m F♯m7 B7
Yet she's true, like ice, like fire
E
People carry roses
B A E
Make promises by the hours
B A C
My love she laughs like the flowers
F♯m A E
Valen - tines can't buy her

Verse 2

E
In the dime stores and bus stations
B A E
People talk of situ - ations
B A E
Read books, repeat quo - tations
F♯m F♯m7 B7
Draw con - clusions on the wall
E
Some speak of the future
B A E
My love she speaks softly

cont.

```
B      A                                E
   She knows there's no success like failure
             F#m                   A      E
And that failure's no suc - cess at all
```

Verse 3

```
E
The cloak and dagger dangles
B  A                         E
         Madams light the candles
B  A                            E
         In ceremonies of the horsemen
             F#m          F#m7   B7
Even the pawn must hold a grudge
E
Statues made of matchsticks
B  A                              E
         Crumble into one an - other
B     A                           E
   My love winks, she does not bother
      F#m                       A         E
She knows too much to argue or to judge
```

Instrumental

E	E B	A	E B

A	E	A B	E	E ‖

Verse 4

```
E
The bridge at midnight trembles
B  A                          E
         The country doctor rambles
B  A                               E
         Bankers' nieces seek per - fection
               F#m                 F#m7      B7
Expecting all the gifts that wise men bring
     E
The wind howls like a hammer
B  A                               E
         The night blows cold and rainy
B  A                             E
         My love she's like some raven
           F#m               A        E
At my window with a broken wing
```

Outro

A	E	A	E ‖ *To fade*

LOVE SICK

Words & Music by Bob Dylan

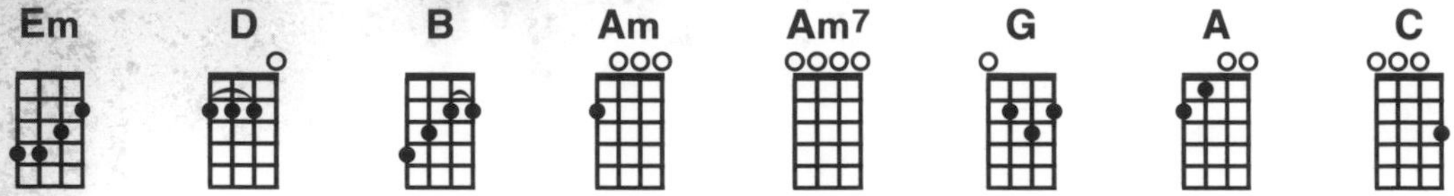

Verse 1

Em D Em
I'm walking through streets that are dead

D Em
Walking, walking with you in my head

D B Am Am7
My feet are so tired, my brain is so wired

Em
And the clouds are weeping

Verse 2

Em D Em
Did I hear someone tell a lie?

D Em
Did I hear someone's distant cry?

D B Am Am7
I spoke like a child; you de - stroyed me with a smile

Em
While I was sleeping

Chorus 1

G A G A Em
I'm sick of love but I'm in the thick of it

G A G A Em
This kind of love I'm so sick of it

Verse 3

Em D Em
I see, I see lovers in the meadow

D Em
I see, I see silhouettes in the window

D B Am Am7
I watch them 'til they're gone and they leave me hanging on

Em
To a shadow

Chorus 2

G A G A Em
I'm sick of love; I hear the clock tick
G A G A Em
This kind of love; I'm love sick

Instrumental

: Em	Em	D	D
Em	Em	Em	Em :
Am	Am7	Am7
Em	Em	Em	Em	

Verse 4

Em D Em
Sometimes the silence can be like the thunder
D Em
Sometimes I feel like I'm being plowed under
D B Am Am7
Could you ever be true? I think of you
Em
And I wonder

Chorus 3

G A G A Em
I'm sick of love; I wish I'd never met you
G A G A Em
I'm sick of love; I'm trying to for - get you

Outro

Em D
Just don't know what to do
C B Em
I'd give anything to be with you

MAGGIE'S FARM

Words & Music by Bob Dylan

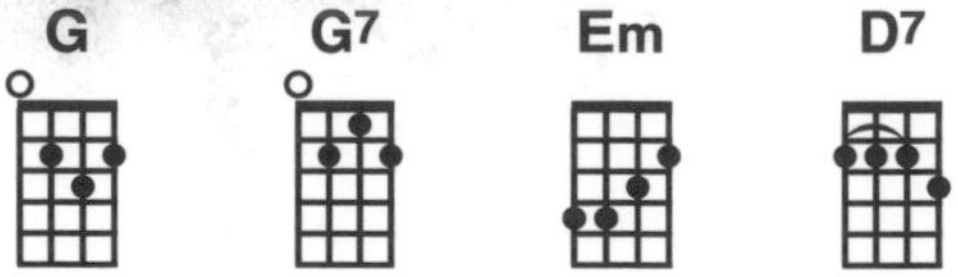

Intro | G | G ‖

Verse 1

```
G7
I ain't gonna work on Maggie's farm no more

No, I ain't gonna work on Maggie's farm no more

Well, I wake in the morning, fold my hands and pray for rain

I got a head full of ideas that are drivin' me insane
    Em                                     D7
It's a shame the way she makes me scrub the floor
 G7
I ain't gonna work on Maggie's farm no more
```

Link 1 | G | G ‖

Verse 2

```
G7
I ain't gonna work for Maggie's brother no more

No, I ain't gonna work for Maggie's brother no more

Well, he hands you a nickel, he hands you a dime

He asks you with a grin if you're havin' a good time
      Em                                D7
Then he fines you every time you slam the door
 G7
I ain't gonna work for Maggie's brother no more
```

Link 2 | G | G ‖

Verse 3

```
G7
I ain't gonna work for Maggie's pa no more

No, I ain't gonna work for Maggie's pa no more

Well, he puts his cigar out in your face just for kicks

His bedroom window it is made out of bricks
    Em                              D7
The National Guard stands around his door
    G7
Ah, I ain't gonna work for Maggie's pa no more
```

Link 3

| G | G | G | G ‖

Verse 4

```
G7
I ain't gonna work for Maggie's ma no more

No, I ain't gonna work for Maggie's ma no more

Well, she talks to all the servants about man and God and law

Everybody says she's the brains behind pa
     Em                                  D7
She's sixty-eight, but she says she's twenty - four
 G7
I ain't gonna work for Maggie's ma no more
```

Link 4

| G | G | G ‖

Verse 5

```
G7
I ain't gonna work on Maggie's farm no more

No, I ain't gonna work on Maggie's farm no more

Well, I try my best to be just like I am

But everybody wants you to be just like them
          Em                            D7
They say sing while you slave and I just get bored
 G7
I ain't gonna work on Maggie's farm no more
```

Outro

| G | G | G | G ‖ *To fade*

MAKE YOU FEEL MY LOVE

Words & Music by Bob Dylan

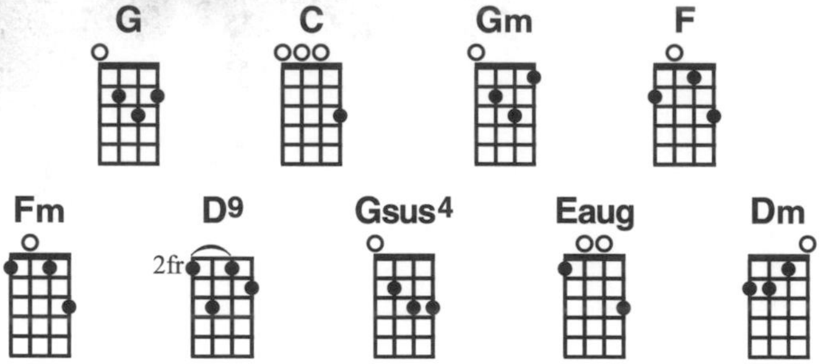

To match original recording, tune ukulele up a semitone

Verse 1

G C G
When the rain is blowing in your face
Gm F
And the whole world is on your case
Fm C
I could offer you a warm embrace
D9 G11 C
To make you feel my love

Verse 2

C G
When the evening shadows and the stars appear
Gm F
And there is no one there to dry your tears
Fm C
I could hold you for a million years
D9 G11 C
To make you feel my love

Bridge 1

F C
I know you haven't made your mind up yet
Eaug F C
But I would never do you wrong
F C
I've known it from the moment that we met
Dm G
No doubt in my mind where you be - long

```
             C                     G
Verse 3        I'd go hungry, I'd go black and blue
             Gm                              F
               I'd go crawling down the avenue
             Fm                         C
               There's nothing that I wouldn't do
             D9                 Gsus4  C
               To make you feel my love


Instrumental | C       | G       | Gm         | F       |

             | Fm      | C       | D9  Gsus4  | C       ||


             Fm                                C
Bridge 2       The storms are raging on the rollin' sea
             Eaug                            C
               And on the highway of re - gret
             F                                    C
               The winds of change are blowing wild and free
             Dm                                   Gsus4
             You ain't seen nothing like me yet


             C                                       G
Verse 4      I could make you happy, make your dreams come true
             Gm                F
               Nothing that I wouldn't do
             Fm                          C
               Go to the ends of the earth for you
             D9                 Gsus4  C
               To make you feel my love


Outro        | C       | G       | Gm         | F       |

             | Fm      | C       | D9  Gsus4  | C       ||  To fade
```

MAMA, YOU BEEN ON MY MIND

Words & Music by Bob Dylan

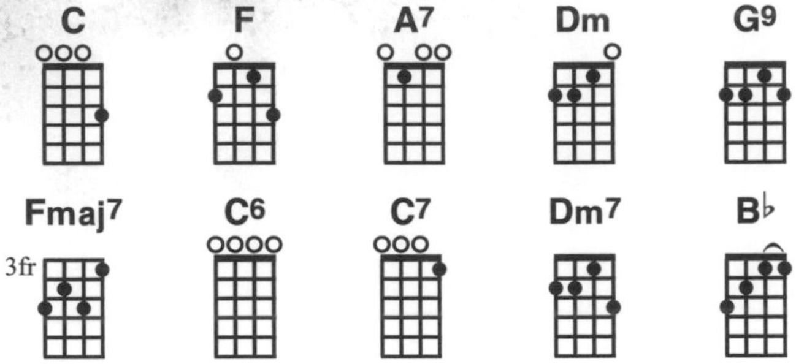

To match original recording, tune ukulele up a semitone

Intro | C | C |

Verse 1

```
  F                                 A7
Perhaps it's the color of the sun cut flat
   Dm          G9
An' cov'rin' the crossroads I'm standing at
  F              Fmaj7  Dm  C              F
Or maybe it's the weather or  something like that
                     C6  C7  F
But mama, you been on  my  mind
```

Verse 2

```
F                                          A7
I don't mean trouble, please don't put me down or get upset
          Dm        G9
I am not pleadin' or sayin', "I can't forget"
 F              A7          Dm        Dm7      B♭
I do not walk the floor bowed down an' bent, but yet
F               C6  C7   F
Mama, you been on my   mind
```

Verse 3

```
         F
Even though my mind is hazy an' my thoughts they might be narrow
               A7                    Dm        G9
Where you been don't bother me nor bring me down in sorrow
    F            C                                Dm        Dm7      B♭
It don't even matter to me where you're wakin'  up    tomorrow
      F                     C6    C7   F
But mama, you're just on  my mind
```

Verse 4

```
           F
I am not askin' you to say words like "yes" or "no"
         A7     Dm            G9
Please understand me, I got no place for you t'go
           F                C           Dm                Dm7      B♭
I'm just breathin' to myself, pretendin' not that I don't know
F                    C6   C7   F       C
Mama, you been on  my mind
```

Instrumental

```
| F          A7 | Dm            | G9            | F      C      |
| Dm  Dm7  B♭   | F      C7     | F       C     | C7     N.C.   |
```

Verse 5

```
              F
When you wake up in the mornin', baby, look inside your mirror
      A7                                         Dm        Dm7        G9
You know I won't be next to you, you know I won't be near
           F              A7                    Dm        Dm7      B♭
I'd just be curious to know if you can see yourself as clear
     F                     C7                  F       C    C7   F
As someone who has had you on his mind
```

THE MAN IN ME

Words & Music by Bob Dylan

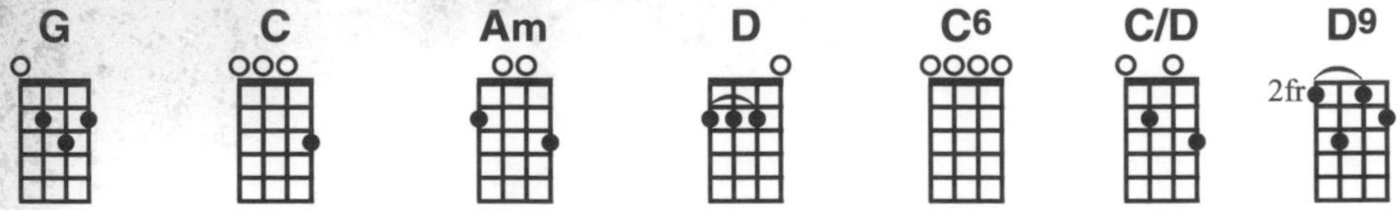

To match original recording, tune ukulele up a semitone

Intro | G | C Am | D | G |
| G | C | D | G ||

Verse 1
G C G Am
The man in me will do nearly any task
D C C6 G
And as for compen - sation, there's little he would ask

Take a woman like you
C C/D G
To get through to the man in me

Verse 2
G C G Am
Storm clouds are raging all a - round my door
D C C6 G
I think to my - self I might not take it any more

Take a woman like your kind
C C/D G
To find the man in me

Chorus 1
Am G
But, oh, what a wonderful feeling
Am G
Just to know that you are near
Am G
Sets my heart a-reeling
Am D
From my toes up to my ears

Verse 3

```
    G                                     C          G      Am
The man in me will hide sometimes to keep from bein' seen
    D                       C                  C6                   G
But that's just because he doesn't want to turn into some ma - chine

Took a woman like you
       C                C/D      G
To get through to the man in me
```

Outro ‖: G | C G | Am | D D9 | G :‖ *Repeat to fade*

MASTERS OF WAR

Words & Music by Bob Dylan

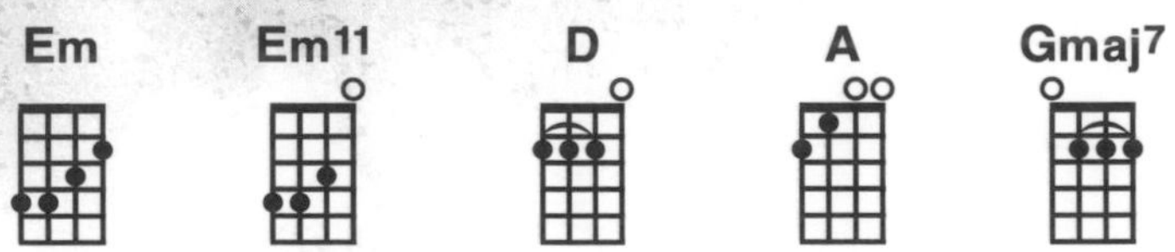

To match recording, tune ukulele up a semitone

Verse 1

```
| Em   Em11 |
Em                     Em11  Em    Em11
Come you masters of       war
Em                Em11  Em   Em11
You that build all the guns
Em                    Em11 Em     Em11
You that build the death planes
Em                    Em11 Em     Em11
You that build the big    bombs
Em                    Em11 Em    Em11
You that hide be - hind  walls
Em                    Em11 Em    Em11
You that hide be - hind  desks
Em                  D
I just want you to know
                         Em     Em11
I can see through your masks
```

Verse 2

```
Em                       Em11  Em    Em11
You that never have done  nothin'
Em             Em11  Em   Em11
But build to de  -  story
Em                Em11 Em     Em11
You play with my    world
Em       D          Em   Em11
Like it's your little toy
```

cont.

```
Em                 Em11 Em   Em11
You put a gun in my    hand
Em        D            Em   Em11
And you hide from my eyes
Em                      D
And you turn and run farther
                        Em   Em11
When the fast bullets fly
```

Verse 3

```
Em          Em11 Em   Em11
Like Judas of     old
Em           Em11  Em   Em11
You lie and de  -  ceive
Em                 Em11 Em   Em11
A world war can be      won
Em         D           Em   Em11
You want me to be - lieve
Em                  Em11 Em   Em11
But I see through your   eyes
Em    D                   Em   Em11
And I see through your brain
Em                      Gmaj7
Like I see through the water
      D                Em    Em11 Em Em11
That runs down my drain
```

Verse 4

```
Em          Em11 Em      Em11
You fasten the    triggers
Em              Em11 Em   Em11
For the others to___ fire
Em                   Em11   Em    Em11
Then you set back and___ watch
Em        D           Em          Em11
When the death count gets higher
Em           Em11 Em      Em11
You hide in your  mansion
Em        D           A    Em    Em11
While the young peo - ple's blood
Em                     D
Flows out of their bodies
                       Em   Em11
And is buried in the mud
```

Verse 5

Em Em11 Em Em11
You've thrown the worst fear

Em Em11 Em Em11
That can ever be hurled

Em Em11 Em Em11 Em
Fear to bring children

D A Em Em11
Into the world

Em Em11 Em Em11
For threatening my baby

Em D A Em Em11
Un - born and un - named

Em Gmaj7
You ain't worth the blood

D Em Em11
That runs in your veins

Verse 6

Em Em11 Em Em11
How much do I know

Em Em11 Em Em11
To talk out of turn

Em Em11 Em Em11
You might say that I'm young

Em D Em Em11
You might say I'm un - learned

Em Em11 Em Em11
But there's one thing I know

Em D Em Em11
Though I'm younger than you

Em D
Even Jesus would never

A Em Em11
Forgive what you do

Verse 7

Em Em11 Em Em11
Let me ask you one question

Em Em11 Em Em11
Is your money that good

Em Em11 Em Em11
Will it buy you for - giveness

Em D A Em Em11
Do you think that it could

Em Em11 Em Em11
I think you will find

cont.

```
Em     D                    A  Em   Em11
When your death takes its toll
Em                D
All the money you made
              A               Em  Em11
Will never buy back your soul
```

Verse 8

```
Em                 Em11  Em   Em11
And I hope that you     die
Em                   Em11 Em   Em11
And your death'll come soon
Em              Em11 Em    Em11
I will follow your casket
Em    D       A    Em    Em11
In the pale af - ter - noon
Em                      Em11   Em      Em11
And I'll watch while you're lowered
Em       D   A     Em  Em11
Down to your death - bed
Em                    Gmaj7
And I'll stand o'er your grave
         D                Em
'Til I'm sure that you're dead
```

MILLION DOLLAR BASH

Words & Music by Bob Dylan

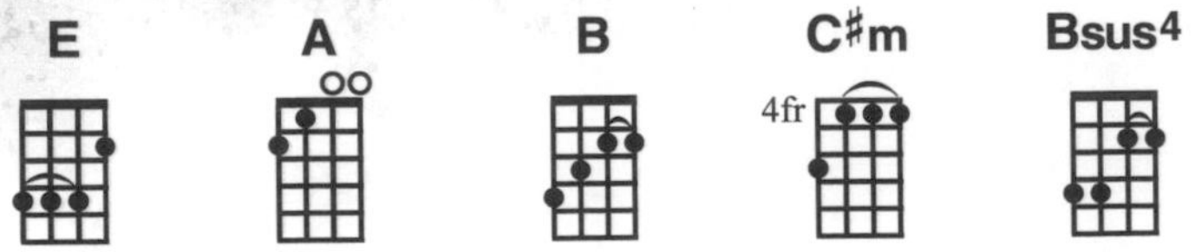

Intro | E | E ||

Verse 1

E
Well, that big dumb blonde
A
With her wheel in the gorge
E
And Turtle, that friend of theirs
B
With his checks all forged
E
And his cheeks in a chunk
A
With his cheese in the cash
E
They're all gonna be there
B E
At that million dollar bash
C♯m A E
Ooh, baby, ooh - ee
C♯m A E
Ooh, baby, ooh - ee
Bsus4 E
It's that million dollar bash

```
                E
Verse 2         Ev'rybody from right now
                   A
                To over there and back
                    E
                The louder they come
                    B
                The harder they crack
                E
                Come now, sweet cream
                A
                Don't forget to flash
                                 E
                We're all gonna meet
                               B          E
                At that million dollar bash
                C#m        A    E
                Ooh, baby, ooh - ee
                C#m        A    E
                Ooh, baby, ooh - ee
                        Bsus4      E
                It's that million dollar bash

                E
Verse 3         Well, I took my counselor
                A
                Out to the barn
                    E
                Silly Nelly was there
                    B
                She told him a yarn
                         E
                Then a - long came Jones
                A
                Emptied the trash
                E
                Ev'rybody went down
                        B          E
                To that million dollar bash
                C#m        A    E
                Ooh, baby, ooh - ee
                C#m        A    E
                Ooh, baby, ooh - ee
                        Bsus4      E
                It's that million dollar bash
```

Verse 4

E
Well, I'm hittin' it too hard
A
My stones won't take
E
I get up in the mornin'
B
But it's too early to wake
E
First it's hello, goodbye
A
Then push and then crash
E
But we're all gonna make it
A E
At that million dollar bash
C♯m A E
Ooh, baby, ooh - ee
C♯m A E
Ooh, baby, ooh - ee
Bsus4 E
It's that million dollar bash

Verse 5

E
Well, I looked at my watch
A
I looked at my wrist
E B
Punched myself in the face

With my fist
E
I took my potatoes
A
Down to be mashed
E
Then I made it over
B E
To that million dollar bash
C♯m A E
Ooh, baby, ooh - ee
C♯m A E
Ooh, baby, ooh - ee
Bsus4 E
It's that million dollar bash *To fade*

MISSISSIPPI

Words & Music by Bob Dylan

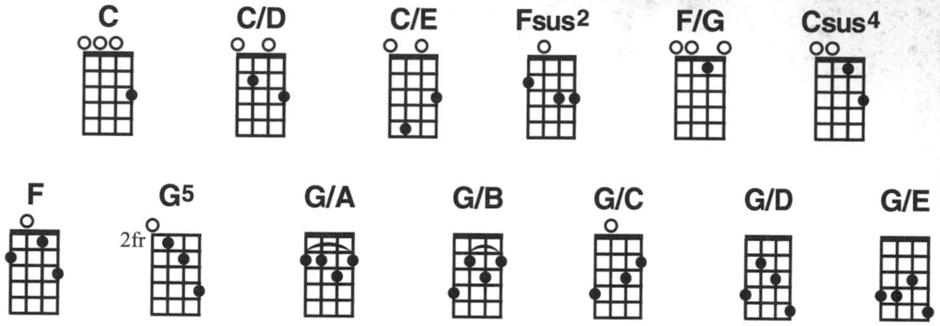

Intro | C C/D C/E | F/G C ||

Verse 1

```
C                       Csus4   C
Every step of the way          we walk the line
                                        F
Your days are numbered, so are mine
C                    F  C                    F
Time is pilin' up, we struggle and we scrape
C          C/D          C/E  Fsus2   F/G              C
We're all boxed in,                  nowhere to es - cape
C                Csus4  C
City's just a jungle; more games to play
                 Csus4       C                    F
Trapped in the heart of it, tryin' to get a - way
      C               F               C                F
I was raised in the country, I been workin' in the town
C     C/D   C/E           Fsus2             F/G      C
I been     in trouble ever since I set my suitcase down
```

Chorus 1

```
G5                     G/A  G/B           G/C
Got nothin' for you, I had nothin' before
G/D                    G/E                F          G5
Don't even have anything for my - self any - more
               G/A    G/B           G/C
Sky full of fire,    pain pourin' down
G/D                   G/E          F            G5
Nothing you can sell me, I'll see you a - round
```

cont.

C Csus4 C
All my powers of ex - pression and thoughts so sublime
Csus4 C F
Could never do you justice in reason or rhyme
C F C F
Only one thing I did wrong
C C/D C/E Fsus2 F/G C
Stayed in Mississip - pi a day too long

Link 1

| C C/D C/E Fsus2 | F/G C |

Verse 2

C Csus4
Well, the devil's in the alley, mule's in the stall
C Csus4 F
Say anything you wanna, I have heard it all
C F C F
I was thinkin' 'bout the things that Rosie said
C C/D C/E Fsus2 F/G C
I was dreaming I was sleepin' in Rosie's bed
C Csus4 C Csus4
Walkin' through the leaves, falling from the trees
C Csus4 C F
Feelin' like a stranger nobody sees
C F C F
So many things that we never will un - do
C C/D C/E Fsus2 F/G C
I know you're sorry, I'm sorry too

Chorus 2

G5 G/A G/B G/C
Some people will offer you their hand and some won't
G/D G/E F G5
Last night I knew you, to - night I don't
G/A G/B G/C
I need somethin' strong to distract my mind
G/D G/E F G5
I'm gonna look at you 'til my eyes go blind
C Csus4 C Csus4
Well I got here followin' the southern star
C F
I crossed that river just to be where you are
C F C F
Only one thing I did wrong
C C/D C/E Fsus2 F/G C
Stayed in Mississip - pi a day too long

Link 2 | C C/D C/E Fsus2 | F/G C |

Verse 3

```
C                                Csus4   C                 Csus4
Well my ship's been split to splinters and it's sinkin' fast
C                       Csus4           C               F
I'm drownin' in the poison, got no future, got no past
C                      Csus4 C                 Csus4
But my heart is not weary, it's light and it's free
C        C/D           C/E        Fsus2                   F/G       C
I've got nothin' but affection for all those who've sailed with me
C             Csus4  C                            Csus4
Everybody movin' if they ain't already there
C             Csus4        C       F
Everybody got to move some - where
C                 F     C                      F
Stick with me baby, stick with me any - how
C                 C/D         C/E        Fsus2 F/G        C
Things should start to get interest - in'      right about now
```

Chorus 3

```
G5                G/A   G/B        G/C
My clothes are wet,   tight on my skin
G/D                   G/E          F                G5
Not as tight as the corner that I painted myself in
               G/A       G/B        G/C
I know that fortune is waitin' to be kind
G/D                 G/E       F          G5
So give me your hand and say you'll be mine
```

Verse 4

```
C                          Csus4   C            Csus4
Well, the emptiness is endless, cold as the clay
C                  Csus4                 C                       F
You can always come back, but you can't come back all the way
C          F     C     F
Only one thing I did wrong
C           C/D          C/E  Fsus2  F/G      C
Stayed in Mississip - pi         a      day too long
```

Outro | C C/D C/E Fsus2 | F/G C ||

MOST LIKELY YOU GO YOUR WAY AND I'LL GO MINE

Words & Music by Bob Dylan

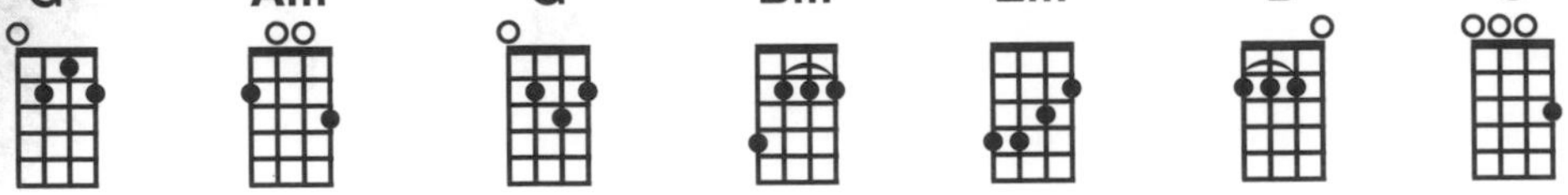

Intro | G7 | G7 | G7 | G7 ||

Verse 1

Am
You say you love me and you're thinkin' of me
G7
But you know you could be wrong
Am
You say you told me that you wanna hold me
G
But you know you're not that strong
Bm Em
I just can't do what I done before
Am
I just can't beg you anymore
G G7 D
I'm gonna let you pass and I'll go last
G Bm C G
Then time will tell just who fell
C D N.C
And who's been left behind
G7
When you go your way and I go mine

Verse 2

Am
You say you disturb me and you don't deserve me
G7
But you know sometimes you lie
Am
You say you're shakin' and you're always achin'
G7
But you know how hard you try

cont.

Bm Em
Sometimes it gets so hard to care
Am
It can't be this way ev'rywhere
G G7 D
And I'm gonna let you pass, yes, and I'll go last
G Bm C D
Then time will tell just who fell
C D
And who's been left behind
D7 N.C
When you go your way and I go mine

Bridge

Em
The judge, he holds a grudge
D
He's gonna call on you
Em
But he's badly built and he walks on stilts
D
Watch out he don't fall on you

Link

| G7 | G7 | G7 | G7 ||

Verse 3

Am
You say you're sorry for tellin' stories
G7
That you know I believe are true
Am
You say ya got some other kinda lover
G7
And yes, I believe you do
Bm
You say my kisses are not like his
Am
But this time I'm not gonna tell you why that is
G D
I'm just gonna let you pass, yes, and I'll go last
G Bm C G C D N.C.
Then time will tell who fell and who's been left behind
G7
When you go your way and I go mine

Outro

|: G7 | G7 | G7 | G7 :| *Repeat to fade*

MOST OF THE TIME

Words & Music by Bob Dylan

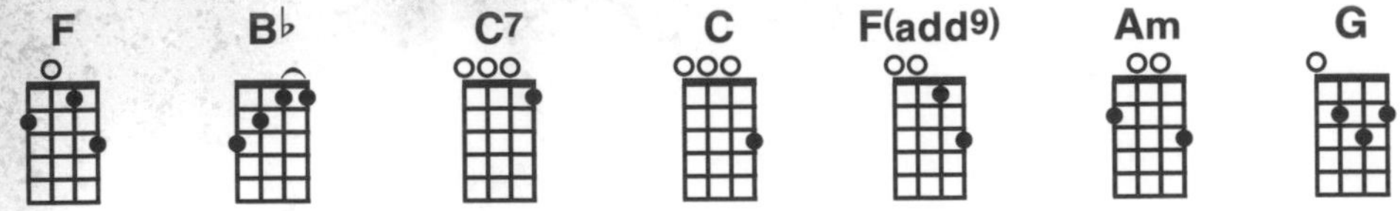

Intro | F | B♭ | C7 | F ||

Verse 1

```
                      C          F(add9)
Most of the time I'm clear focused all around
                     C                       F(add9)
Most of the time I can keep both feet on the ground
Am                         G  F
I can follow the path, I can read the signs
Am                    G F
Stay right with it when the road unwinds
                         C                      F(add9)
I can handle whatever I stumble upon
                   Am     G     F
I don't even notice she's gone
                        C   F   C   F
Most of the time
```

Verse 2

```
                        C  F(add9)
Most of the time it's well understood
                         C  F(add9)
Most of the time I wouldn't change it if I could
Am                                  G   F
I can make it all match up, I can hold my own
Am                                  G   F
I can deal with the situation right down to the bone
               C                   F(add9)
I can survive, I can endure
                             Am    G      F
And I don't even think about her
                        C  F(add9)  C  F(add9)
Most of the time
```

Verse 3

C F(add9)
Most of the time my head is on straight
C F(add9) G
Most of the time I'm strong enough not to hate
Am G F G
I don't build up illusion 'til it makes me sick
Am G F
I ain't afraid of confusion no matter how thick
C F(add9)
I can smile in the face of mankind
Am G F(add9)
Don't even remember what her lips felt like on mine
C F C F G
Most of the time

Verse 4

Am G C G
Most of the time she ain't even in my mind
Am G
I wouldn't know her if I saw her
C
She's that far behind
E7 Am E7
Most of the time I can't even be sure if she was ever with me
Am F/C
Or if I was with her

Verse 5

C F(add9)
Most of the timc I'm halfway content
C F(add9) C
Most of the time I know exactly where it went
Am G F
I don't cheat on myself, I don't run and hide
Am F
Hide from the feelings that are buried inside
C F(add9)
I don't compromise and I don't pretend
Am F(add9)
I don't even care if I ever see her again
C F(add9)
Most of the time

Outro ‖: C | F(add9) | C | F(add9) :‖ *Repeat to fade*

MR. TAMBOURINE MAN

Words & Music by Bob Dylan

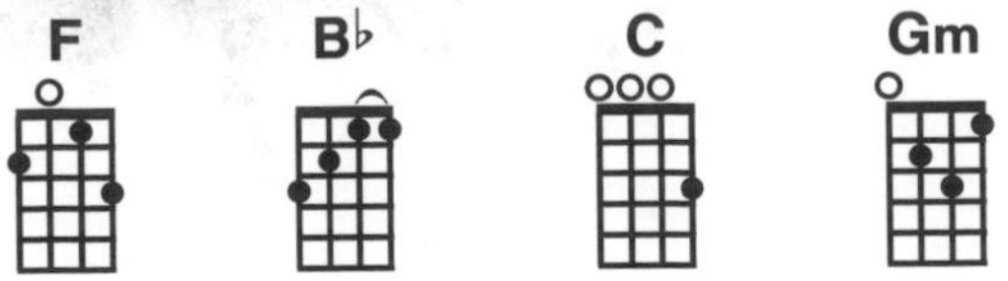

Intro | F | F ||

Chorus 1

B♭ C F B♭
Hey! Mr. Tambourine Man, play a song for me
F B♭ C
I'm not sleepy and there is no place I'm going to
B♭ C F B♭
Hey! Mr. Tambourine Man, play a song for me
F B♭ C F
In the jingle jangle morning I'll come followin' you

Verse 1

B♭ C F B♭
Though I know that evenin's empire has returned into sand
F B♭
Vanished from my hand
F B♭ Gm C
Left me blindly here to stand but still not sleeping
B♭ C F B♭
My weariness amazes me, I'm branded on my feet
F B♭
I have no one to meet
F B♭ Gm C
And the ancient empty street's too dead for dreaming

Chorus 2 As Chorus 1

Link 1 | F | F ||

Verse 2

B♭ C F B♭
Take me on a trip upon your magic swirlin' ship
F B♭ F B♭
My senses have been stripped, my hands can't feel to grip
F B♭
My toes too numb to step
F Gm C
Wait only for my boot heels to be wanderin'
B♭ C F B♭
I'm ready to go anywhere, I'm ready for to fade
F B♭ F B♭
Into my own parade, cast your dancing spell my way
Gm C
I promise to go under it

Chorus 3

B♭ C F B♭
Hey! Mr. Tambourine Man, play a song for me
F B♭ C
I'm not sleepy and there is no place I'm going to
B♭ C F B♭
Hey! Mr. Tambourine Man, play a song for me
F B♭ C F
In the jingle jangle morning I'll come followin' you

Link 2

| F | F ‖

Verse 3

B♭ C
Though you might hear laughin', spinnin'
F B♭
Swingin' madly across the sun
F B♭ F B♭
It's not aimed at anyone, it's just escapin' on the run
F B♭ Gm C
And but for the sky there are no fences facin'
B♭ C F B♭
And if you hear vague traces of skippin' reels of rhyme
F B♭ F B♭
To your tambourine in time, it's just a ragged clown behind
F B♭
I wouldn't pay it any mind
F Gm C
It's just a shadow you're seein' that he's chasing

Chorus 4 As Chorus 3

Harmonica Break

| B♭ C | F B♭ | F B♭ | F B♭ | F B♭ |

| F B♭ | F Gm | C | B♭ C | F B♭ |

| F B♭ | F B♭ | F Gm | C F | F ||

Verse 4

B♭ C F B♭
Then take me disappearin' through the smoke rings of my mind
F B♭ F B♭
Down the foggy ruins of time, far past the frozen leaves
F B♭ F B♭
The haunted, frightened trees, out to the windy beach
F B♭ Gm C
Far from the twisted reach of crazy sorrow
B♭ C F
Yes, to dance beneath the diamond sky with one hand waving free
F B♭ F B♭
Silhouetted by the sea, circled by the circus sands
F B♭ F B♭
With all memory and fate driven deep beneath the waves
F Gm C
Let me forget about today until tomorrow

Chorus 5 As Chorus 3

Coda | B♭ C | F B♭ | F B♭ | F B♭ | F B♭ || *To fade*

MY BACK PAGES

Words & Music by Bob Dylan

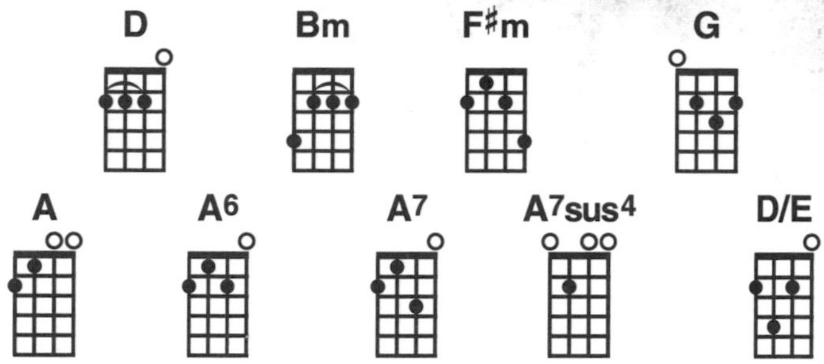

To match recording, tune ukulele up a semitone

Intro | D | D | D | D ||

Verse 1

D Bm F♯m
Crimson flames tied through my ears
G A A6 A7 D
Rollin' high and migh - ty traps
Bm F♯m D
Pounced with fire on flaming roads
G F♯m A A6
Using ideas as my maps
A7 G Bm A A6 A7 D
"We'll meet on edges, soon," said I
Bm G A
Proud 'neath heated brow
D Bm D
Ah, but I was so much older then
G A A6 A7 D A A6 A7 A7sus4
I'm younger than that now

Verse 2

D Bm F♯m
Half-wracked prejudice leaped forth
G A A6 A7 D
"Rip down all hate," I screamed
Bm F♯m
Lies that life is black and white
G A A6 A7
Spoke from my skull. I dreamed

```
            Bm               F#m
cont.       Ro - mantic facts of musketeers
               G                          A
            Foun - dationed deep, some - how
                D      Bm        F#m  G
cont.       Ah, but I was so much older then
              A         A6  A7        D
            I'm young - er   than that now

            D           Bm          F#m
Verse 3     Girls' faces formed the forward path
                G       A     A6    A7  D
            From phony jea - lou - sy
                            Bm    F#m
            To memo - rizing politics
               G       D/E     A    A6   A7
            Of ancient histo - ry
                 Bm                   F#m
            Flung down by corpse e - vangelists
               G                               A    A6    A7
            Un - thought of, though, some - how
                D                   G      D
            Ah, but I was so much older then
               G          A     A6  A7  D
            I'm younger than       that now

            D           Bm           F#m
Verse 4     A self - or - dained pro - fessor's tongue
               G         A  A6   A7  D
            Too serious           to  fool
                       Bm      F#m
            Spouted out that liberty
              G                 A        A6  A7
            Is just equality in school
                 Bm         F#m
            "E - quality," I spoke the word
               G                 A   A6    A7
            As if a wedding vow
                D      Bm
            Ah, but I was so much older then
               G          A     A6  A7  D
            I'm younger than       that now
```

Verse 5

D Bm F♯m
In a soldier's stance, I aimed my hand

G A A6 A7 D
At the mongrel dogs who teach

Bm F♯m
Fearing not that I'd become my e - nemy

G A A6 A7
In the instant that I preach

Bm G D
My pathway led by confusion boats

Bm F♯m A A6 A7
Mutiny from stern to bow

D Bm G D
Ah, but I was so much older then

A A6 A7 D
I'm young - er than that now

Verse 6

D Bm F♯m
Yes, my guard stood hard when abstract threats

G A A6 A7 D
Too noble to ne - glect

Bm F♯m
Deceived me into thinking

G A A6 A7
I had something to protect

Bm F♯m
Good and bad, I de - fine these terms

G A A6 A7
Quite clear, no doubt, some - how

D Bm G D
Ah, but I was so much older then

A A6 A7 D
I'm young - er than that now

NOT DARK YET

Words & Music by Bob Dylan

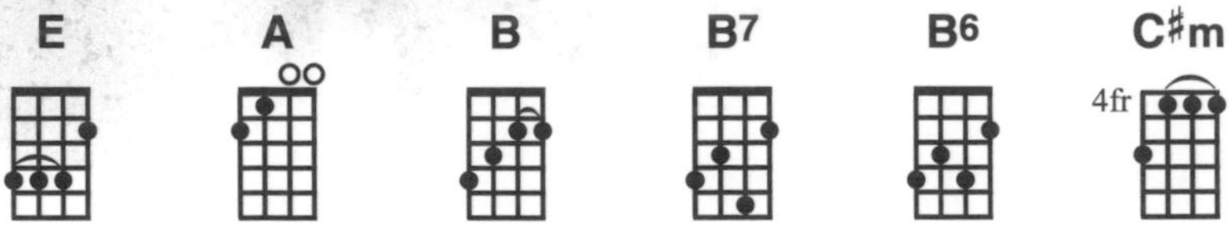

Intro | E | A E | E | E A | E | E | E ||

Verse 1

E A E
Shadows are falling and I've been here all day
A E
It's too hot to sleep, time is running away
B B7 B6 E
Feel like my soul has turned into steel
C♯m B A E
I've still got the scars that the sun didn't heal
B B7 B6 E
There's not even room enough to be anywhere
C♯m B A E
It's not dark yet, but it's getting there

Link 1 | E | E ||

Verse 2

E A E
Well, my sense of humanity has gone down the drain
A E
Behind every beautiful thing there's been some kind of pain
B B7 B6 E
She wrote me a letter and she wrote it so kind
C♯m B A E
She put down in writing what was in her mind
B B7 B6 E
I just don't see why I should even care
C♯m B A E
It's not dark yet, but it's getting there

Link 2 | E | E ||

Verse 3

```
E                                    A                          E
   Well, I've been to London   and I've been to gay   Paree
                                 A                    E
 I've followed the river   and I got to the sea
B                              B7             B6                  E
   I've been down on the bottom of a world full of lies
C#m                        B        A                E
   I ain't looking for nothing   in anyone's eyes
B                     B7                B6                E
   Sometimes my burden seems more than I can bear
C#m                B    A                          E
   It's not dark yet,   but it's getting there
```

Link 3

| E | A E | E | E A | E |

| B B7 | B6 E | E C#m | B A | E |

| B B7 | B6 E | E C#m | B A | E | E ||

Verse 4

```
E                                          A                    E
   I was born here and I'll die here   against my will
                                      A                  E
I know it looks like I'm moving,   but I'm standing   still
B                               B7            B6            E
   Every nerve in my body is so        vacant and numb
           C#m                            B                      A                E
I can't even remember what it was I came here to   get away from
B                   B7      B6               E
   Don't even hear a murmur of a prayer
C#m                B    A            E
   It's not dark yet,   but it's getting there
```

Coda

| E | E | A E | E | E A | E |

| B B7 | B6 E | E C#m | B A | E |

| B B7 | B6 E | E C#m | B A | E ||

OH, SISTER

Words by Bob Dylan & Jacques Levy
Music by Bob Dylan

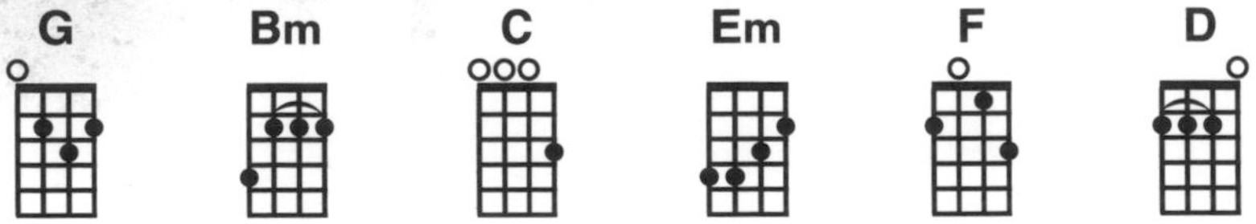

Intro

```
|: G      | Bm     | C      | G      |
|  G      | Em     | C      | G      :|
```

Verse 1

```
G              Bm                C            G
   Oh, sister, when I come to lie in your arms
                 Em              C      G
You should not treat me like a stran - ger
             Bm                  C                G
Our Father would not like the way that you act
                Em          C      G
And you must realize the dan - ger
```

Instrumental 1

```
|: G      | Bm     | C      | G      |
|  G      | Em     | C      | G      :|
```

Verse 2

```
G             Bm          C            G
Oh, sister, am I not a brother to you
                Em               C     G
And one de - serving of af - fec - tion?
             Bm                C                 G
And is our purpose not the same on this earth
                Em              C     G
To love and follow His di - rec - tion?
```

Instrumental 2 As Instrumental 1

Bridge

```
F               C
We grew up to - gether
         G
From the cradle to the grave
   F                  C
We died and were re - born
               G         D
And then mys - teriously saved
```

Verse 3

```
G              Bm             C             G
   Oh, sister, when I come to knock on your door
               Em                 C     G
Don't turn a - way, you'll create sor - row
           Bm          C           G
Time is an ocean but it ends at the shore
                Em      C     G
You may not see me to - mor - row
```

Outro

```
|: G   | Bm  | C   | G   |
|  G   | Em  | C   | G  :|
```

ON A NIGHT LIKE THIS

Words & Music by Bob Dylan

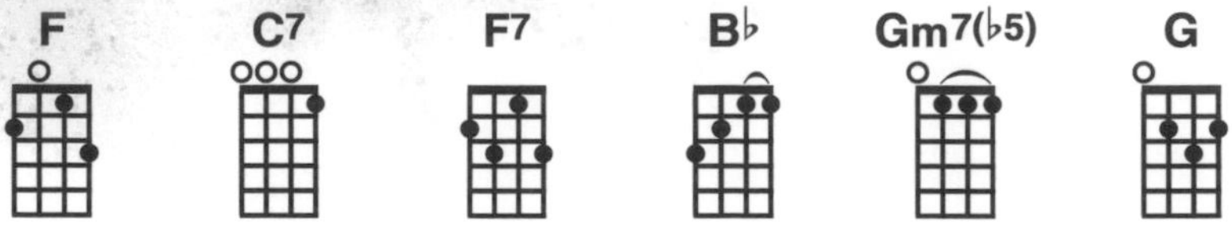

Verse 1

N.C. F
On a night like this

C7
So glad you came around

Hold on to me so tight

F
And heat up some coffee grounds

F7
We got much to talk about

B♭ Gm7♭5
And much to reminisce

F
It sure is right

C7 F
On a night like this

Verse 2

N.C. F
On a night like this

C7
So glad you've come to stay

Hold on to me, pretty miss

F
Say you'll never go a - way to stray

F7
Run your fingers down my spine

B♭ Gm7♭5
Bring me a touch of bliss

F
It sure feels right

C7 F
On a night like this

```
          N.C.          F
Verse 3   On a night like this
                    C7
          I can't get any sleep

          The air is so cold outside
                    F
          And the snow's so deep
                         F7
          Build a fire, throw on logs
             B♭          Gm7♭5
          And listen to it hiss
                     F             C7
          And let it burn, burn, burn, burn
                        F
          On a night like this

          B♭
Bridge    Put your body next to mine
              F
          And    keep me company
          G
          There is plenty a-room for all
            C7
          So    please don't elbow me

          N.C.               F
Verse 4   Let the four winds blow
                            C7
          Around this old cabin door

          If I'm not too far off
                               F
          I think we did this once before
                                      F7
          There's more frost on the window glass
              B♭               Gm7♭5
          With each new tender kiss
                             F
          But it sure feels right
          C7                 F
             On a night like this


Outro     |: F   | F   | C7  | C7    | C7 | C7 | F | F    |

          | F    | F7  | B♭  | Gm7♭5 | F  | C7 | F | F   :|
                                             Repeat to fade
```

ONE MORE CUP OF COFFEE (VALLEY BELOW)

Words & Music by Bob Dylan

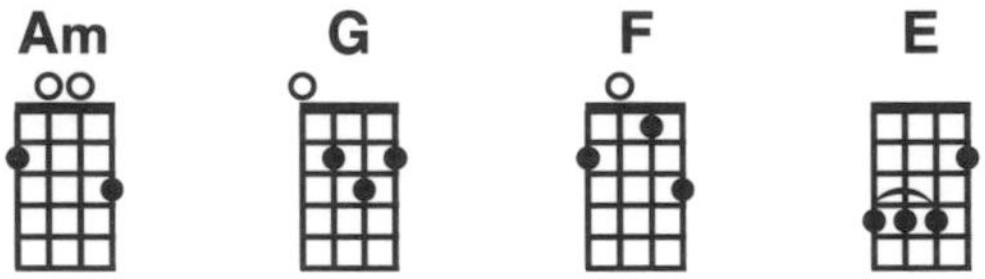


```
Intro        | Am     ||

             |: Am    | G     | F     | E     :|

             | Am     | Am    ||


             Am
Verse 1      Your breath is sweet
                                G
             Your eyes are like two jewels in the sky
             F
                Your back is straight, your hair is smooth
                    E
             On the pillow where you lie
             Am                           G
                But I don't sense affection

             No gratitude or love
             F
                Your loyalty is not to me
                E
             But  to the stars above


             F                              E
Chorus 1     One more cup of coffee for the road
             F                              E
             One more cup of coffee 'fore I go
                                (Am)
             To the valley be - low


Link 1       | Am     | G     | F     | E     ||
```

Verse 2

```
(E)    Am
Your daddy he's an outlaw
         G
And a wanderer by trade
F
   He'll teach you how to pick and choose
      E
And how to throw the blade
Am
   He oversees his kingdom
G
So no stranger does intrude
     F
His voice it trembles as he calls out
          E
For an - other plate of food
```

Chorus 2 As Chorus 1

Link 2 As Link 1

Verse 3

```
(E)    Am
Your sister sees the future
G
Like your mama and yourself
F
  You've never learned to read or write
          E
There's no books upon your shelf
Am
And your pleasure knows no limits
        G
Your voice is like a meadowlark
            F
But your heart is like an ocean
E
Mysterious and dark
```

Chorus 3 As Chorus 1

Outro ‖: Am | G | F | E :‖ Am ‖

ONE OF US MUST KNOW (SOONER OR LATER)

Words & Music by Bob Dylan

F   B♭   Csus4   Dm   Am   Gm   C

```
Intro       | F     B♭ | F     B♭ | F     B♭ | F     B♭ ||

            (B♭) F          B♭  F              B♭  F
Verse 1     I    didn't mean    to treat you so   bad
            B♭              F            Csus4
            You shouldn't take it so personal
              F              B♭  F              B♭  F
            I didn't mean      to make you so   sad
            B♭         F                     Csus4
            You just happened to be there, that's all
            Dm                                   Am
              When I saw you say "goodbye"   to your friend and smile
            Gm                               F
              I thought that it was well   understood
            Dm                                     Am
              That you'd be comin' back in a little while
            Gm                                          B♭                C
              I didn't know that you were sayin' "goodbye" for good

            (B♭) F            C      B♭              F
Chorus 1    But, sooner or later, one of us must know
            B♭              F                          C
              You just did what you're sup - posed to do
            F              C      B♭              F
            Sooner or later, one of us must know
                      B♭      F                C
            That I  really did try to get close to you

Link 1      | F     B♭ | F     B♭ ||
```

Verse 2

```
F                Bb  F                     Bb     F
   I couldn't see      what you could show me
          Bb          F           Csus4
Your scarf had kept your mouth well hid
 F              Bb  F                    Bb     F
I  couldn't see      how you could know me
           Bb           F                      Csus4
But you said you knew me and I be - lieved you did
Dm                          Am
   When you whispered in my ear
Gm                                         F
   And asked me if I was leavin' with you or her
Dm                        Am
   I didn't realize just what I did hear
Gm                          Bb                C
   I didn't realize how young you were
```

Chorus 2

```
(C)   F           C      Bb               F
But, sooner or later, one of us must know
Bb             F                             C
   You just did what you're sup - posed to do
F           C     Bb                  F
Sooner or later, one of us must know
Bb               F              C
That I really did try to get close to you
```

Link 2

```
| F    Bb  | F    Bb  | F    Bb  ||
```

Verse 3

```
F                Bb F                    Bb      F
I couldn't see       when it started snow - in'
         Bb          F        Csus4
Your voice was all that     I heard
F               Bb F                   Bb   F
I  couldn't see       where we were go - in'
     Bb              F            Csus4
But you said you knew an' I     took your word
Dm                                        Am
And then you told me later, as I a - pologized
                         Gm                                F
That you were just kiddin' me, you weren't really  from the farm
Dm                           Am
   An' I told you, as you clawed out my eyes
    Gm                                 Bb          F
That I never really meant to do you   any harm
```

```
Chorus 3     (C)  F          C      B♭                  F
             But, sooner or later, one of us must know
             B♭          F                         C
                You just did what you're sup - posed to do
             F           C      B♭                  F
             Sooner or later, one of us must know
             B♭                      F           C
                That I really did try to get close to you

Outro        | F   C  | B♭   F  | B♭  F  | C        |

             | F   C  | B♭   F  | B♭  F  | C        | F        ||
```

POSITIVELY 4TH STREET

Words & Music by Bob Dylan

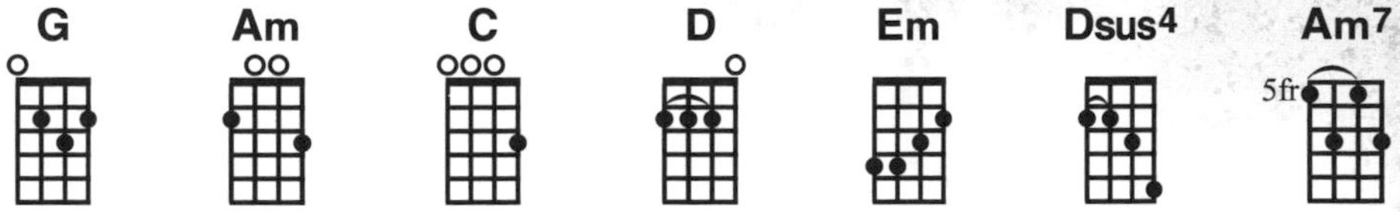

To match original recording, tune ukulele down a semitone

Intro | G | G | G | G ||

Verse 1

```
G              Am
   You got a lotta nerve
   C                  G
To say you are my friend
              D
When I was down
C         Em          D
You just stood there grinning
```

Verse 2

```
G              C
   You got a lotta nerve
                                      G
To say you got a helping hand to lend
           D         C
You just want to be on
    Em          A
The side that's winning
```

Verse 3

```
G              Am
   You say I let you down
    C                    G
You know it's not like that
              D
If you're so hurt
C         Em          D
Why then don't you show it
```

Verse 4

G Am
You say you lost your faith
C G
But that's not where it's at
D
You have no faith to lose
C Em D
And you know it

Verse 5

G Am
I know the reason
C G
That you talk behind my back
D C Em
I used to be among the crowd
D
You're in with

Verse 6

G Am
Do you take me for such a fool
C G
To think I'd make contact
D
With the one who tries to hide
C Em D Dsus4
What he don't know to begin with

Verse 7

G Am
You see me on the street
C G
You always act surprised
D C
You say, "How are you?" "Good luck"
Em D Dsus4
But you don't mean it

Verse 8

G Am
When you know as well as me
C G
You'd rather see me paralyzed
D C Em
Why don't you just come out once
D Dsus4
And scream it

Verse 9

```
 G                Am
   No, I do not feel that good
                  C                      G
When I see the heartbreaks you embrace
            D       C
If I was a master thief
    Em         D          Dsus4
Perhaps I'd rob them
```

Verse 10

```
     G                       Am
And now I know you're dissatisfied
                 C                G
With your position and your place
            D      C
Don't you understand
    Em        D          Dsus4
It's not my problem
```

Verse 11

```
G                   Am
   I wish that for just one time
               C                 G
You could stand inside my shoes
                D         C
And just for that one moment
Em       D        Dsus4
I could be you
```

Verse 12

```
   G                    Am
Yes, I wish that for just one time
               C                G
You could stand inside my shoes
                 D        C       Em
You'd know what a drag it is
    D        Dsus4
To see you
```

Coda

```
||: G        | Am7      | C        | G        |
|   G   D    | C   Em   | D        | Dsus4    :||   Repeat to fade
```

ONE TOO MANY MORNINGS

Words & Music by Bob Dylan

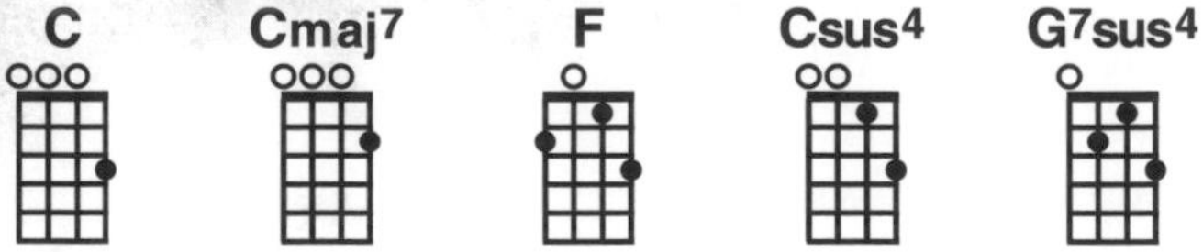

Intro | C | C ||

Verse 1

```
C                                    Cmaj7        F                  C
   Down the street the dogs are barkin' and the day is a-gettin' dark
                   Csus4 C                           G7sus4  C
As the night comes in a - fallin' the dogs'll lose their bark
G7sus4    C                    Cmaj7           F                     C
   An' the silent night will shatter from the sounds inside my mind
                Csus4 C                    G7sus4  C   G7sus4    C
For I'm one too many  mornings and a thousand miles      be - hind
```

Instrumental 1

```
| C        | Cmaj7     | F        | C        |
| C        | C         | C        | G7sus4   | G7sus4 |
| C        | Cmaj7     | F        | C        |
| C        | C  Csus4  | C        | G7sus4   |
| C        | F         | C        | C        ||
```

Verse 2

C Cmaj7 F C
From the crossroads of my doorstep my eyes they start to fade
Csus4 C G7sus4
As I turn my head back to the room where my love and I have laid
C G7sus4 C Cmaj7 F C
An' I gaze back to the street, the sidewalk and the sign
Csus4 C G7sus4 C G7sus4 C
And I'm one too many mornings an' a thousand miles be - hind

Instrumental 2

| C | Cmaj7 | F | C |

| C | C | C | C |

| G7sus4 | G7sus4 |

| C | Cmaj7 | F | C |

| C | C | C | G7sus4 | C G7sus4 |

| C | F | C | C ||

Verse 3

C Cmaj7 F C
It's a restless hungry feeling that don't mean no one no good
Csus4 C G7sus4
When ev'rything I'm a - sayin', you can say it just as good
C G7sus4 C Cmaj7 F C
You're right from your side, I'm right from mine
Csus4 C
We're both just one too many mornings
G7sus4 C G7sus4 C F
An' a thousand miles be - hind

Outro

| C | Cmaj7 | F | C |

| C | C | C | C |

| G7sus4 | G7sus4 |

| C | Cmaj7 | F | C |

| C | C | C | G7sus4 |

| G7sus4 | C | G7sus4 | C ||

PRETTY SARO

Traditional
Arranged by Bob Dylan

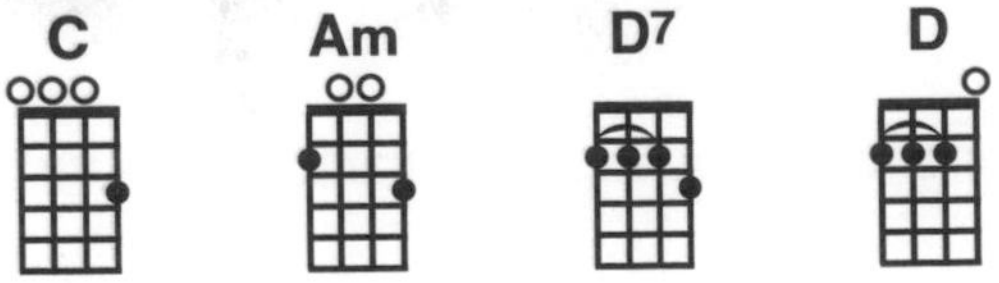

Intro | C C | G ||

Verse 1

G Am
Down in some lone valley
D7 G C G
In a sad lonesome place
Am
Where the wild birds do warble
D
Their notes to in - crease
G C G
Farewell pretty Saro
Am D
I bid you a - dieu
Am
But I dream of pretty Saro
G
Wherever I go

Link 1 | C | C | G ||

Verse 2

```
G                        Am
   Well my love she won't have me
    D7     G
So I under - stand
                  Am
She wants a free - holder
                       D
Who owns a house and land
               Am
I cannot main - tain her
               G      C  G
With silver and gold
              Am
And all of the fine things
       D            G
That a big house can hold
```

Verse 3

```
G           Am
   If I was a    poet
           D7         G      C  G
And could write a fine hand
                 Am
I'd write my love a letter
                 D
That she'd under - stand
                 Am
And write it by the river
                       G      C  G
Where the waters over - flow
                   Am
But I dream of pretty Saro
           D
Wherever I go
```

Outro

| D | D | D | D |

| G ||

QUINN THE ESKIMO (THE MIGHTY QUINN)

Words & Music by Bob Dylan

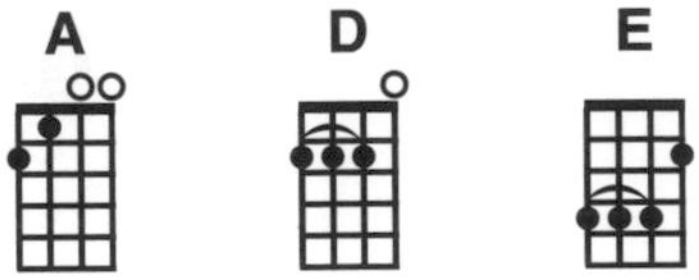

Intro | A | A | A | A ||

Verse 1

A   D   A
Ev'rybody's building the big ships and the boats
                          D
Some are building monuments
A   D
Others, jotting down notes
A   D
Ev'rybody's in despair
A   D
Ev'ry girl and boy
             A   E
But when Quinn the Eskimo gets here
        D   A
Ev'rybody's gonna jump for joy

Chorus 1

|: A   D   A
Come all without, come all within
                     E   D   A
You'll not see nothing like the mighty Quinn :|

Verse 2

A   D   A   D
I like to do just like the rest, I like my sugar sweet
A   D
But guarding fumes and making haste
A   D
It ain't my cup of meat

cont.

```
A               D
   Ev'rybody's 'neath the trees
A                  D
Feeding pigeons on a limb
            A                   E
But when Quinn the Eskimo gets here
     D                      A
All the pigeons gonna run to him
```

Chorus 2

```
   A                    D          A
𝄆 Come all without, come all within
                 E                 D       A
You'll not see nothing like the mighty Quinn 𝄇
```

Solo

```
| A   D  | A   D  | A   D  | A   D  |
| A   D  | A   D  | A   E  | D   A  ||
```

Verse 3

```
A                                    D      A                 D
   A cat's meow and a cow's moo, I   can recite 'em all
A                          D
   Just tell me where it hurts yuh, honey
         A                       D
And I'll tell you who to call
A                   D
   Nobody can get no sleep
                       A                  D
There's someone on ev'ryone's toes
            A                   E
But when Quinn the Eskimo gets here
          D                          A
Ev'rybody's gonna wanna doze
```

Chorus 3

```
   A                    D          A
𝄆 Come all without, come all within
                 E                 D       A
You'll not see nothing like the mighty Quinn 𝄇
```

Coda

```
| A   E  | D   A  ||
```

RAINY DAY WOMEN #12 & 35

Words & Music by Bob Dylan

F7 B♭7 C7

Intro | F7 | F7 | F7 | F7 | B♭7 | B♭7 |

| F7 | F7 | C7 | C7 | F7 | F7 ||

Verse 1

F7
Well, they'll stone ya when you're trying to be so good

They'll stone ya just a-like they said they would

B♭7
They'll stone ya when you're tryin' to go home

F7
Then they'll stone ya when you're there all alone

C7
But I would not feel so all alone

F7
Everybody must get stoned

Well, they'll stone ya when you're walkin' 'long the street

They'll stone ya when you're tryin' to keep your seat

B♭7
They'll stone ya when you're walkin' on the floor

F7
They'll stone ya when you're walkin' to the door

C7
But I would not feel so all alone

F7
Everybody must get stoned

Verse 2

F7
They'll stone ya when you're at the breakfast table

They'll stone ya when you are young and able

B♭7
They'll stone ya when you're tryin' to make a buck

cont.

F7
They'll stone ya and then they'll say, "good luck"
C7
Tell ya what, I would not feel so all alone
F7
Everybody must get stoned

Instrumental 1

F7	F7	F7	F7	B♭7	B♭7
F7	F7	C7	C7	F7	F7

F7
Verse 3 Well, they'll stone you and say that it's the end

Then they'll stone you and then they'll come back again
B♭7
They'll stone you when you're riding in your car
F7
They'll stone you when you're playing your guitar
C7
Yes, but I would not feel so all alone

Everybody must get stoned

Instrumental 2

F7	F7	F7	F7	B♭7	B♭7
F7	F7	C7	C7	F7	F7

F7
Verse 4 Well, they'll stone you when you walk all alone

They'll stone you when you are walking home
B♭7
They'll stone you and then say you are brave
F7
They'll stone you when you are set down in your grave
C7
But I would not feel so all alone
F7
Everybody must get stoned

Outro

F7	F7	F7	F7	
B♭7	B♭7	F7	F7	*Fade out*

ROLL ON JOHN

Words & Music by Bob Dylan

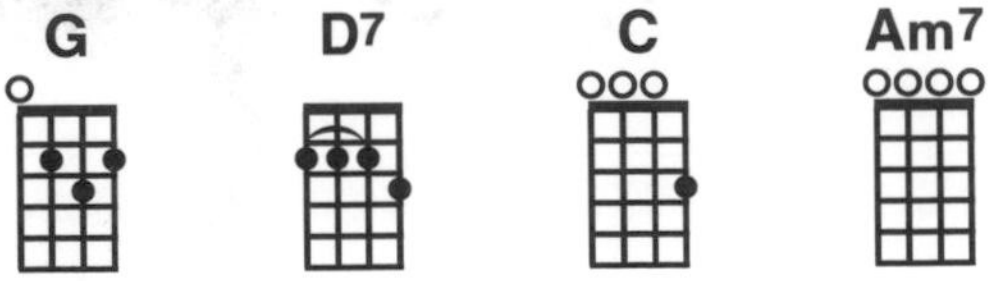

Intro

G	D7	G	G
C	C	G	C
D7	Am7	G	

Verse 1

```
G                                  C
Doctor, doctor, tell me the time of day
                                        G
Another bottle's empty, another penny spent
                                        C
He turned around and he slowly walked a - way
                                         G
They shot him in the back and down he went
```

Chorus 1

```
G          C
Shine your light
       D7
Move it on
             C
You burned so bright
       G
Roll on, John
```

Verse 2

```
G                                                   C
From the Liverpool docks to the red light Hamburg streets
                                    G
Down in the quarry with the Quarrymen
                                                C
Playing to the big crowds, playing to the cheap seats
                                                        G
Another day in the life on your way to your journey's end
```

Chorus 2 As Chorus 1

Verse 3

G Sailing through the trade winds bound for the South C
Rags on your back just like any other slave G
They tied your hands and they clamped your mouth C
Wasn't no way out of that deep, dark cave G

Chorus 3 As Chorus 1

Verse 4

G I heard the news today, oh boy C
They hauled your ship up on the shore G
Now the city gone dark, there is no more joy C
They tore the heart right out and cut it to the core G

Chorus 4 As Chorus 1

Verse 5

G Put down your bags and get 'em packed C
Leave right now, you won't be far from wrong G
The sooner you go, the quicker you'll be back C
You been cooped up on an island far too long G

Chorus 5 As Chorus 1

Verse 6

G Slow down, you're moving way too fast C
Come together right now over me G
Your bones are weary, you're about to breathe your last C
Lord, you know how hard that it can be G

Chorus 6 As Chorus 1

Verse 7

```
G                                        C
Roll on John, roll through the rain and snow
                                                    G
Take the right hand road and go where the buffalo roam
                                           C
They'll trap you in an ambush 'fore you know
                         G
Too late now to sail back home
```

Chorus 7 As Chorus 1

Verse 8

```
G                   C
Tyger, tyger, burning bright
                          G
I pray the Lord my soul to keep
                     C
In the forest of the night
                           G
Cover him over, and let him sleep
```

Chorus 8 As Chorus 1

Outro 𝄆 G | C | C | G 𝄇 *Repeat to fade*

Señor (Tales Of Yankee Power)

Words & Music by Bob Dylan

Am(add9) Am Em F C Cmaj7 G Dm

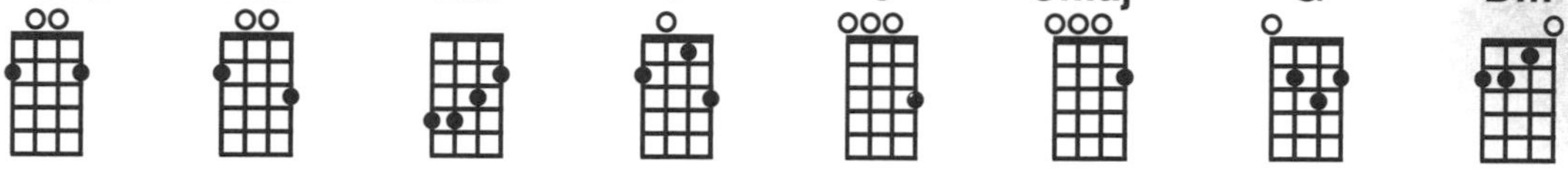

Intro |: Am(add9) | Am(add9) | Am(add9) | Am(add9) :|

Verse 1

```
        Am      Em          F                    C
Se - ñor, se - ñor, do you know where we're headin'?
                           Cmaj7          Am
Lincoln County Road        or Arma - geddon?
                      G                     F      Em  Dm
Seems like I been down this way be - fore
                                 Am
Is there any truth in that, se - ñor?
```

Verse 2

```
        Am      Em          F                       C
Se - ñor, se - ñor, do you know where she is hidin'?
                           Cmaj7     Am
How long are we gonna be ridin'?
                                G                   F
How long must I keep my eyes glued to the door?
Em             Dm                             Am
   Will there be any comfort there, se - ñor?
```

Bridge 1

```
(Am)      C                                  Em
There's a wicked wind still blowin' on that upper deck
              F                                     Am
There's an iron cross still hangin' down from a - round her neck
              C                                  Em
There's a marchin' band still playin' in that vacant lot
              F                                               Am
Where she held me in her arms one time and said, "For - get me not"
```

Verse 3

```
Am          Em          F                    C
Señor, se - ñor, I can see that painted wagon
                       Cmaj7 Am
I can smell the tail of the dragon
                     G              F
Can't stand the suspense any - more
Em          Dm                                  Am
   Can you tell me who to contact here, se - ñor?
```

Instrumental 1

Am	Am	Em	Em
F	C	C Cmaj7	Am
Am	G	F	F Em
Dm	Dm	Am	Am

Bridge 2

```
(Am)     C                                  Em
Well, the last thing I remember before I stripped and kneeled
               F                                      Am
Was that trainload of fools bogged down in a magnetic field
  C                                 Em
A gypsy with a broken flag and a flashing ring
       F                                              Am
Said, "Son, this ain't a dream no more, it's the real thing"
```

Verse 4

```
    Am       Em                        F                  C
Se - ñor, se - ñor, you know their hearts is as hard as leather
                    Cmaj7          Am
Well, give me a minute, let me get it together
              G                    F
I just gotta pick myself up off the floor
Em  Dm                              Am
         I'm ready when you are, se - ñor
```

Instrumental 2 As Instrumental 1

Verse 5

```
        Am        Em        F                  C
Se - ñor, se - ñor, let's disconnect these cables
         Cmaj7      Am
Over - turn these tables
                                 G                  F
This place don't make sense to me no more
Em           Dm                                          Am
   Can you tell me what we're waiting for, se - ñor?
```

Instrumental 3

Am	Am	Em	Em
F	C	C Cmaj7	Am
Am	G	F	F Em
Dm	Dm	Am	Am

Outro

Am(add9)	Am(add9)	Am(add9)	Am(add9)

SAD-EYED LADY OF THE LOWLANDS

Words & Music by Bob Dylan

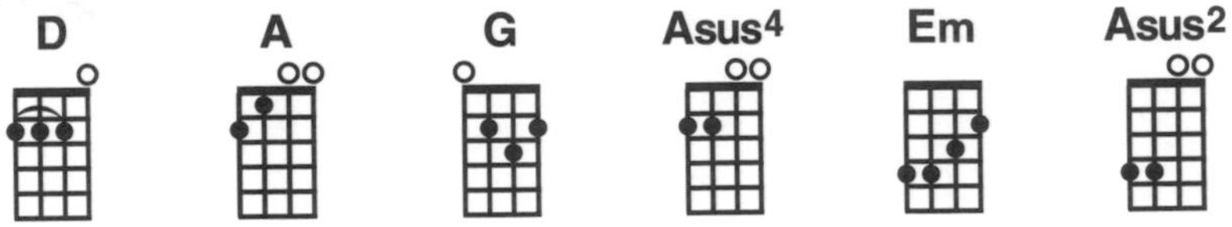


```
Intro      |: D       | A        | G        | Asus4 A :|

                          D       A              G           Asus4  A
Verse 1    With your mercury mouth in the missionary times
                       D        A                  G              Asus4  A
           And your eyes like smoke and your prayers like rhymes
           G                D                     A        D
           And your silver cross, and your voice like chimes
                                            Em          Asus4  A      Asus2  A
           Oh, who among them do they think could bury you?
                          D        A           G         Asus4  A
           With your pockets well pro - tected at last
                          D       A                      G               Asus4  A
           And your streetcar visions which you place on the grass
                          G        D                    A        D
           And your flesh like silk, and your face like glass
                                                 Em    Asus4  A      Asus2  A
           Who among them do they think could carry you?

           Em                         D    A
Chorus 1   Sad-eyed lady of the low - lands
           Em                                        D      A
           Where the sad-eyed prophet says that no man comes
               D      A     G     A   G     D     Asus4  A
           My ware - house eyes, my Ara - bian drums
           Em                                  Asus4  A     Asus2  A
           Should I leave them by your gate?
              Em                      D
           Or, sad-eyed lady, should I wait?
```

Verse 2

A G Asus4 A
With your sheets like metal and your belt like lace
D A G Asus4 A
And your deck of cards missing the jack and the ace
G D A D
And your basement clothes and your hollow face
Em Asus4 A Asus2 A
Who among them can think he could out - guess you?
D A G Asus4 A
With your silhou - ette when the sunlight dims
D A G Asus4 A
Into your eyes where the moonlight swims
G D A D
And your matchbook songs and your gypsy hymns
Em Asus4 A Asus2 A
Who among them would try to impress you?

Chorus 2

Em D A
Sad-eyed lady of the low - lands
Em D A
Where the sad-eyed prophet says that no man comes
D A G A G D Asus4 A
My ware - house eyes, my Ara - bian drums
Em Asus4 A Asus2 A
Should I leave them by your gate
Em D
Or, sad-eyed lady, should I wait?

Verse 3

D A G Asus4 A
The kings of Tyrus with their convict list
D A G Asus4 A
Are waiting in line for their geranium kiss
G D A D
And you wouldn't know it would happen like this
Em Asus4 A Asus2 A
But who among them really wants just to kiss you?
D A G Asus4 A
With your childhood flames on your midnight rug
D A G Asus4 A
And your Spanish manners and your mother's drugs
G D A D
And your cowboy mouth and your curfew plugs
Em Asus4 A Asus2 A
Who among them do you think could resist you?

Chorus 3

```
Em                   D     A
Sad-eyed lady of the low - lands
Em                                  D       A
Where the sad-eyed prophet says that no man comes
    D     A     G     A   G    D   Asus4  A
My ware - house eyes, my Ara - bian drums
Em                          Asus4 A    Asus2 A
Should I leave them by your gate
   Em                     D
Or, sad-eyed lady, should I wait?
```

Verse 4

```
        D               A                   G          Asus4 A
Oh, the farmers and the businessmen, they all did de - cide
   D             A          G                       Asus4 A
To show you the dead angels   that they used to hide
    G                 D      A                     D
But why did they pick you to sympathize with their side?
                    Em         Asus4 A    Asus2 A
Oh, how could they ever mis - take you?
      D             A           G            Asus4 A
They wished you'd accepted the blame for the farm
    D                  A           G              Asus4 A
But with the sea at your feet and the phony false a - larm
              G       D                 A           D
And with the child of a hoodlum wrapped up in your arms
                 Em            Asus4 A    Asus2 A
How could they ever, ever per - suade you?
```

Chorus 4

```
Em                   D     A
Sad-eyed lady of the low - lands
Em                                  D       A
Where the sad-eyed prophet says that no man comes
    D     A     G     A   G    D   Asus4  A
My ware - house eyes, my Ara - bian drums
Em                          Asus4 A    Asus2 A
Should I leave them by your gate
   Em                     D
Or, sad-eyed lady, should I wait?
```

Verse 5

```
D                         A            G          Asus4  A
With your sheet-metal memory of Cannery Row
           D          A              G                         Asus4  A
And your magazine-husband who one day just had to go
           G           D     A                                 D
And your gentleness now, which you just can't help but show
                             Em              Asus4   A   Asus2  A
Who among them do you think would employ you?
D                            A                G         Asus4  A
Now you stand with your thief, you're on his pa - role
           D          A                     G          Asus4  A
With your holy me - dallion which your fingertips fold
           G          D               A          D
And your saintlike face and your ghostlike soul
                   Em                          Asus4   A     Asus2  A
Oh, who among them do you think could destroy you?
```

Chorus 5

```
Em                     D     A
Sad-eyed lady of the low - lands
Em                                        D        A
Where the sad-eyed prophets say that no man comes
    D      A      G      A    G      D     Asus4  A
My ware - house eyes, my Ara - bian drums
Em                              Asus4  A      Asus2  A
Should I leave them by your gate
   Em                          D
Or, sad-eyed lady, should I wait?
```

Outro

```
|: D        | A        | G        | Asus4  A  |
|  D        | A        | G        | Asus4  A  |
|  G        | D        | A        | D         |
|  D        | Em       | Asus4  A | Asus2  A :|   Repeat to fade
```

SARA

Words & Music by Bob Dylan

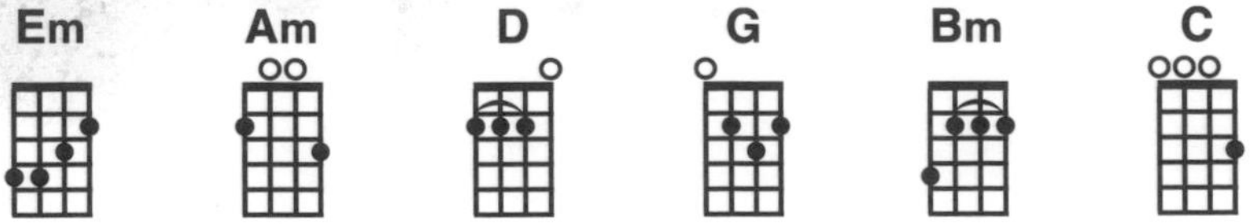

Intro

|: Em | Am | D | Em :|

|: G Bm | C | D | C Em :|

Verse 1

```
Em                Am
I laid on a dune, I looked at the sky
               D                        Em
When the children were babies and played on the beach
                               Am
You came up behind me, I saw you go by
              D                  Em
You were always so close and still within reach
```

Chorus 1

```
G  Bm C
Sara,  Sara
D                          C          Em
Whatever made you want to change your mind?
G  Bm C
Sara,  Sara
  D                   C       Em
So easy to look at, so hard to define
```

Verse 2

```
    Em                              Am
I can still see them playin' with their pails in the sand
     D                   Em
They run to the water their buckets to fill
                                   Am
I can still see the shells fallin' out of their hands
       C                  Em
As they follow each other back up the hill
```

Chorus 2

```
G Bm C
Sara, Sara
D                         C          Em
Sweet virgin angel, sweet love of my life
G Bm C
Sara, Sara
  D            C        Em
Radiant jewel, mystical wife
```

Verse 3

```
Em                         Am
Sleepin' in the woods by a fire at night
C                       Em
Drinkin' white rum in a Portugal bar
                          Am
Them playin' leapfrog and hearin' about Snow White
D                         Em
You in the marketplace in Savanna-la-Mar
```

Chorus 3

```
G Bm C
Sara, Sara
    D                     C     Em
It's all so clear, I could never forget
G Bm C
Sara, Sara
D                               C       Em
Lovin' you is the one thing I'll never regret
```

Verse 4

```
      Em                                Am
I can still hear the sounds of those Methodist bells
    D                      Em
I'd taken the cure and had just gotten through
                           Am
Stayin' up for days in the Chelsea Hotel
         D                    Em
Writin' "Sad-Eyed Lady of the Lowlands" for you
```

Chorus 4

```
G  Bm C
Sara,  Sara
   D                            C          Em
Wherever we travel we're never apart
G   Bm   C
Sara, oh Sara
D                    C               Em
Beautiful lady, so dear to my heart
```

Verse 5

```
Em                         Am
How did I meet you? I don't know
   D                             Em
A messenger sent me in a tropical storm
                                                Am
You were there in the winter, moonlight on the snow
          D                                Em
And on Lily Pond Lane when the weather was warm
```

Chorus 5

```
G   Bm    C
Sara,  oh Sara
D                         C      Em
Scorpio Sphinx in a calico dress
G  Bm C
Sara,  Sara
D                                C          Em
You must forgive me my unworthiness
```

Verse 6

```
             Em                    Am
Now the beach is deserted except for some kelp
          D                            Em
And a piece of an old ship that lies on the shore
                                           Am
You always responded when I needed your help
       D                    Em
You gimme a map and a key to your door
```

Chorus 6

```
G   Bm  C
Sara, oh Sara
D                              C          Em
Glamorous nymph with an arrow and bow
G   Bm  C
Sara, oh Sara
D                        C          Em
Don't ever leave me, don't ever go
```

Outro

```
||: Em       | Am       | D        | Em       :||

||: G   Bm   | C        | D        | C  Em    :||
```

SERIES OF DREAMS

Words & Music by Bob Dylan

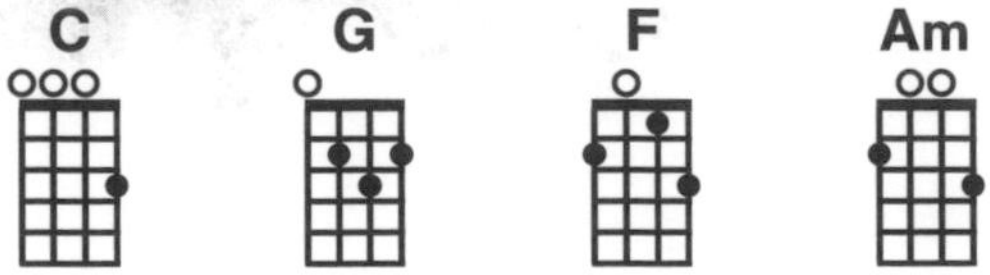

Intro 𝄆 C | C | C | C 𝄇 *Play 3 times*

Verse 1

```
    C        G              C
I was thinking  of a series of dreams
                 G              C
Where nothing  comes up to the top
            G                    C
Everything  stays down where it's wounded
                           F
And comes to a permanent stop
       C
Wasn't thinking of anything specific
                                           F
Like in a dream, when someone wakes up and screams
   C
Nothing too very scientific
             G           C
Just thinking  of a series of dreams
```

Verse 2

```
C        G              C
Thinking  of a series of dreams
                 G              C
Where the time  and the tempo fly
                    G             C
And there's no exit  in any direction
                                       F
'Cept the one that you can't see with your eyes
```

```
                 C
cont.     Wasn't making any great connection
                                                   F
          Wasn't falling for any intricate scheme
            C
          Nothing that would pass inspection
                         G                   C
          Just thinking   of a series of dreams

          Am                F                          C
Bridge 1  Dreams where   the umbrella is folded
          Am   F                         C
          Into     the path you are hurled
                  Am          F                        C
          And the cards are   no good that you're holding
                                                G
          Unless they're from another world

             C     G                C
Verse 3   In one,   numbers were burning
                         G                 C
          In another,   I witnessed a crime
                  G                                    C
          In one,   I was running, and in another
                                                  F
          All I seemed to be doing was climb
                 C
          Wasn't looking for any special assistance
                                                       F
          Not going to any great extremes
                 C
          I'd already gone the distance
                         G                C
          Just thinking   of a series of dreams

          Am                F                          C
Bridge 2  Dreams where   the umbrella is folded
          Am   F                         C
          Into     the path you are hurled
                  Am          F                        C
          And the cards are   no good that you're holding
                                                G
          Unless they're from another world
```

Link 1 | C | G | C | C |

| C | C | F | F |

```
        C
I'd already gone the distance
               G              C
Just thinking  of a series of dreams
```

Link 2 | C | G | C | C |

```
               G              C
Just thinking  of a series of dreams
               G              C
Just thinking  of a series of dreams
```

Coda | C | C | F | F |

| C | C | C | C |

| C | C | F | F || *To fade*

SIMPLE TWIST OF FATE

Words & Music by Bob Dylan

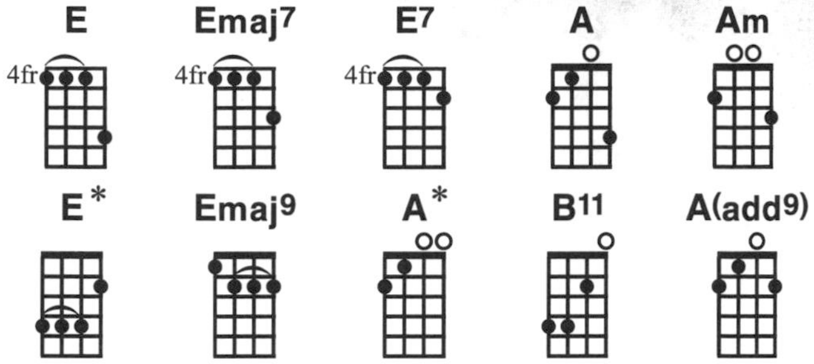

Intro

| E | Emaj7 | E7 | A |
| Am | E* Emaj9 A* | E* B11 | E* ||

Verse 1

E
They sat together in the park
Emaj7
As the evening sky grew dark
E7 A A(add9)
She looked at him and he felt a spark tingle to his bones
Am E* Emaj9 A*
'Twas then he felt alone and wished that he'd gone straight
E* B11 E*
And watched out for a simple twist of fate

Verse 2

E
They walked along by the old canal
Emaj7
A little confused, I remember well
E7 A
And stopped into a strange hotel with a neon burnin' bright
Am E* Emaj9 A*
He felt the heat of the night hit him like a freight train
E* B11 E*
Moving with a simple twist of fate

Verse 3

E
A saxophone someplace far off played
Emaj7
As she was walkin' by the arcade
E7 A
As the light bust through a beat-up shade where he was wakin' up
Am E* Emaj9 A
She dropped a coin into the cup of a blind man at the gate
E* B11 E*
And forgot about a simple twist of fate

Solo

| E | Emaj7 | E7 | A |

| Am | E* Emaj9 A | E* B11 | E* ||

Verse 4

E
He woke up, the room was bare
Emaj7
He didn't see her anywhere
E7 A
He told himself he didn't care, pushed the window open wide
Am E* Emaj9 A*
Felt an emptiness inside to which he just could not relate
E* B11 E*
Brought on by a simple twist of fate

Verse 5

E
He hears the ticking of the clocks
Emaj7
And walks along with a parrot that talks
E7 A
Hunts her down by the waterfront docks where the sailors all come in
Am E* Emaj9 A*
Maybe she'll pick him out again, how long must he wait
E* B11 E*
Once more for a simple twist of fate

Verse 6

```
E
   People tell me it's a sin
Emaj7
   To know and feel too much within
E7                                         A
    I still believe she was my twin, but I lost the ring
Am                                  E*      Emaj9    A*
She was born in spring, but I was born too late
E*                 B11               E*
   Blame it on a simple twist of fate
```

Coda

```
| E          | Emaj7            | E7        | A/E        |
| Am         | E*  Emaj9  A*    | E*   B11  | E*         ||
```

SHE BELONGS TO ME

Words & Music by Bob Dylan

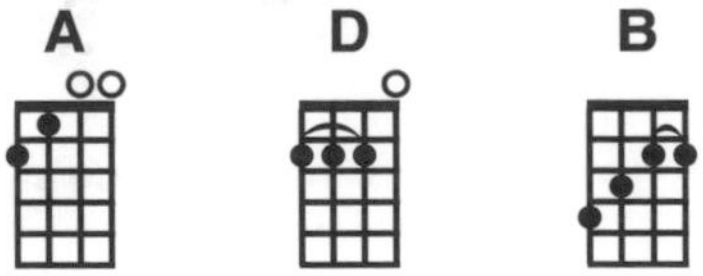

Intro | A ||

Verse 1

```
             A
She's got everything she needs
            D                          A         D    A
She's an artist, she don't look back
             D
She's got everything she needs
                                       A         D    A
She's an artist, she don't look back
                         B
She can take the dark out of the nighttime
       D                        A          D    A
And   paint the daytime black
```

Verse 2

```
             A
You will start out standing
D                                        A         D    A
Proud to steal her anything she sees
             D
You will start out standing
                                         A        D    A
Proud to steal her anything she sees
                    B                                       D
But you will wind up peeking through her keyhole
                        A          D    A
Down upon your knees
```

Verse 3

```
     A
She   never stumbles
       D                A       D    A
She's got no place to fall
     D
She never stumbles
                        A       D   A
She's got no place to fall
        B
She's nobody's child
     D                           A      D     A
The Law can't touch her at all
```

Link

```
| A       | D      | A  D   | A      | D       | D      |
| A  D    | A      | B      | D      | A  D    | A      ||
```

Verse 4

```
                A
She wears an Egyptian ring
  D                    A       D   A
It sparkles before she speaks
                D
She wears an Egyptian ring
                       A       D    A
It sparkles before she speaks
          B
She's a hypnotist collector
    D                  A       D   A
You are a walking antique
```

Verse 5

```
     A
Bow down to her on Sunday
  D                           A        D    A
Salute her when her birthday comes
     D
Bow down to her on Sunday
                              A        D    A
Salute her when her birthday comes
              B
For Halloween give her a trumpet
         D                    A        D    A
And for Christmas, buy her a drum
```

Coda

```
| A       | D      | A  D   | A      ||
                              Fade out
```

SHELTER FROM THE STORM

Words & Music by Bob Dylan

D A6 G

Intro ‖: D | D | D | D :‖

Verse 1

```
D                         A6     G                      D
'Twas in another lifetime, one of toil and blood
                                 A6                G
When blackness was a virtue and the road was full of mud
  D                         A6             G
I came in from the wilderness, a creature void of form
            D                         A6      G                   (D)
"Come in," she said, "I'll give you shelter from the storm"
```

Link 1 | D | A6 | G | D |

| D | A6 | G | D ‖

Verse 2

```
D                        A6               G                 D
And if I pass this way again, you can rest as - sured
                             A6                 G
I'll always do my best for her, on that I give my word
      D                                A6                            G
In a world of steel-eyed death, and men who are fighting to be warm
            D                         A6      G                   (D)
"Come in," she said, "I'll give you shelter from the storm"
```

Link 2 | D | A6 | G | D ‖

```
             D                         A6                  G                D
Verse 3      Not a word was spoke be - tween us, there was little risk in - volved
                              A6                 G
             Everything up to that point had been left unresolved
             D                 A6                    G
               Try imagin - ing a place where it's always safe and warm
                     D                       A6           G                 (D)
             "Come in," she said, "I'll give you      shelter from the storm"

Link 3       As Link 1

             D                         A6        G             D
Verse 4      I was burned out from ex - haustion, buried in the hail
                               A6                 G
             Poisoned in the bushes an' blown out on the trail
             D                  A6             G
               Hunted like a crocodile, ra - vaged in the corn
                     D                       A6     G               (D)
             "Come in," she said, "I'll give you shelter from the storm"

Link 4       As Link 1

             D          A6                   G                 D
Verse 5      Suddenly I turned around and she was standin' there
                                   A6                   G
             With silver bracelets on her wrists and flowers in her hair
                 D                       A6                G
             She walked up to me so gracefully and took my crown of thorns
                     D                       A6     G               (D)
             "Come in," she said, "I'll give you shelter from the storm"

Link 5       As Link 1

             D                       A6       G                    D
Verse 6      Now there's a wall be - tween us, somethin' there's been lost
                                    A6     G
             I took too much for granted, got my signals crossed
                 D                  A6            G
             Just to think that it all began on a long-forgotten morn
                     D                       A6     G               (D)
             "Come in," she said, "I'll give you shelter from the storm"
```

Link 6 As Link 1

Verse 7

D   A6   D   D
Well, the deputy walks on hard nails and the preacher rides a mount
                   A6   G
But nothing really matters much, it's doom alone that counts
        D   A6   G
And the one-eyed under - taker, he blows a futile horn
      D   A6   G   (D)
"Come in," she said, "I'll give you shelter from the storm"

Link 7 As Link 1

Verse 8

D   A6   G   D
I've heard newborn babies wailin' like a mournin' dove
                 A6   G
And old men with broken teeth stranded without love
     D   A6   G
Do I understand your question, man, is it hopeless and forlorn?
      D   A6   G   (D)
"Come in," she said, "I'll give you shelter from the storm"

Link 8 As Link 1

Verse 9

D   A6   G   D
In a little hilltop village, they gambled for my clothes
                      A6   G
I bargained for sal - vation an' they gave me a lethal dose
  D   A6   G
I offered up my innocence and got repaid with scorn
      D   A6   G   (D)
"Come in," she said, "I'll give you shelter from the storm"

Link 9 As Link 1

Verse 10

```
D                                 A6          G                  D
Well, I’m livin’ in a foreign country but I’m bound to cross the line
               A6                   G
Beauty walks a razor’s edge, some - day I’ll make it mine
           D         A6                     G
If I could only turn back the clock to when God and her were born
      D                    A6       G                 (D)
“Come in,” she said, “I’ll give you shelter from the storm”
```

Outro

```
| D   | A6  | G   | D   |
| A6  | G   | G   |
| D   | A6  | G   | G   |
| D   | A6  | G   | G   |
| D   | A6  | G   | D   |
| D   | A6  | G   | G   |
| D   | A6  | G   | G   |
| D   | A6  | G   | G   |
| D   | A6  | G   | G   | D   ||
```

SHOOTING STAR

Words & Music by Bob Dylan

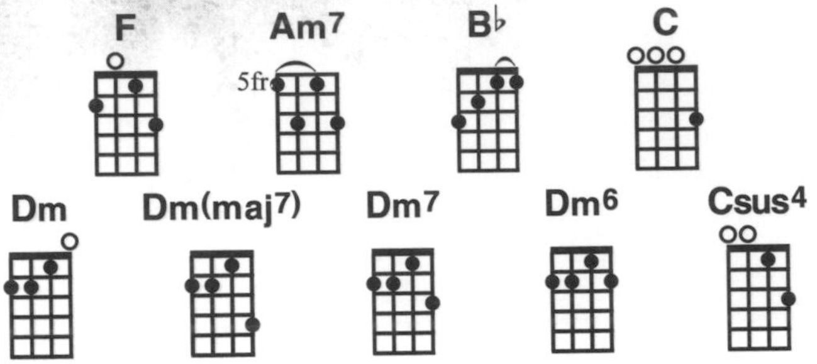

Intro

| F Am7 | B♭ F | F Am7 | B♭ |

| B♭ C | F B♭ | F Am7 | B♭ F ||

Verse 1

F Am7
Seen a shooting star tonight
B♭ F
And I thought of you
Am7
You were trying to break into another world
B♭
A world I never knew
C
I always kind of wondered
F B♭
If you ever made it through
F Am7
Seen a shooting star tonight
B♭ F
And I thought of you

Link

| F Am7 | B♭ F ||

Verse 2

F Am7
Seen a shooting star tonight
B♭ F
And I thought of me

If I was still the same
Am7 B♭
If I ever became what you wanted me to be

cont.

C
Did I miss the mark or overstep the line
F B♭
That only you could see?
F
Seen a shooting star tonight
Am7 B♭ F
And I thought of me

Bridge

Dm Dm(maj7)
Listen to the engine, listen to the bell
Dm7 Dm6
As the last fire truck from hell
B♭
Goes rolling by
C F
All good people are praying
Dm Dm(maj7)
It's the last temptation, the last account
Dm7 Dm6
The last time you might hear the sermon on the mount
B♭ Csus4
The last radio is playing

Verse 3

F Am7
Seen a shooting star tonight
B♭ F
Slip away
Am7
Tomorrow will be
B♭
Another day

C
Guess it's too late to say the things to you
F B♭
That you needed to hear me say
F Am7
Seen a shooting star tonight
B♭ F
Slip away

Coda

| F Am7 | B♭ F | F Am7 | B♭ |
| B♭ C | F B♭ | F Am7 | B♭ F ||

SPANISH HARLEM INCIDENT

Words & Music by Bob Dylan

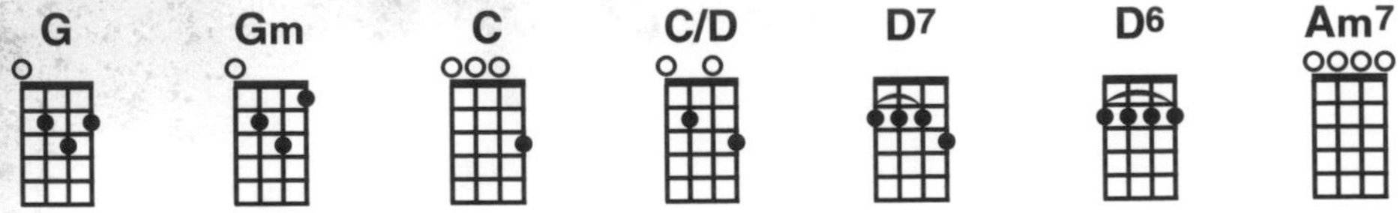


```
Intro      | G  Gm  C   | C    G     | G        ||

Verse 1    Gm     C                    G
           Gypsy gal, the hands of Harlem
           Gm       C                  G
           Cannot hold you to its heat
                Gm          C                            G
           Your tempera - ture's too hot for tam - ing
                Gm          C                  G
           Your flaming feet burn up the street
           C/D  G              C/D         G
           I am homeless, come and take me
           C/D  G                          D7
           Into reach of your rattling drums
                  G              C          D6    D7  G
           Let me know, babe,    all a - bout my fortune
                        C                D6      D7  (G)
           Down a - long my rest - less palms

Link 1     | G    C     | D6     D7  G | G    C     | D6     D7 G |

           | G    C     | G        ||
```

Verse 2

Gm C G
Gypsy gal, you got me swallowed

Gm C G
I have fallen far be - neath

Gm Am7 C G
Your pearly eyes, so fast an' slashing

Gm C G
An' your flashing diamond teeth

C/D G C/D G
The night is pitch black, come an' make my

C/D G C/D D7
Pale face fit into place, ah, please!

G C D6 D7 G
Let me know, babe, I'm near - ly drowning

C D6 D7 (G)
If it's you my life - lines trace

Link 2

| G C | D6 D7 G | G C | D6 D7 G ||

Verse 3

Gm C G
I been wond'rin' all a - bout me

Gm C G
Ever since I seen you there

Gm C G
On the cliffs of your wildcat charms I'm riding

Gm C G
I know I'm 'round you but I don't know where

C/D G C/D G
You have slayed me, you have made me

C/D G C/D D7
I got to laugh half - ways off my heels

G C D6 D7 G
I got to know, babe, will you sur - round me?

C D6 D7 G C G
So I can know if I'm real - ly real

STUCK INSIDE OF MOBILE WITH THE MEMPHIS BLUES AGAIN

Words & Music by Bob Dylan

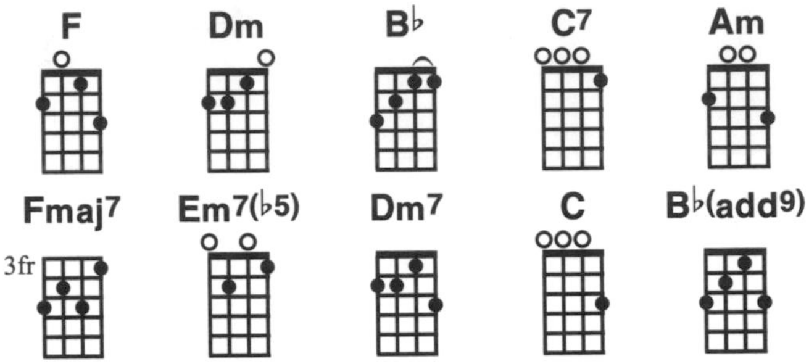

Intro | F | F | F | F ||

Verse 1

F   Dm
Oh, the ragman draws circles
F   Dm
Up and down the block
F   Dm
I'd ask him what the matter was
B♭   C7
But I know that he don't talk
B♭   F
And the ladies treat me kindly
Dm   F
And furnish me with tape
Dm   F
But deep inside my heart
B♭   F
I know I can't escape

Chorus 1

Am
Oh, Mama, can this really be the end
F   Fmaj7   Dm C
To be stuck inside of Mobile
B♭   C7   F
With the Memphis blues again

Verse 2

F   Dm
Well, Shakespeare, he's in the alley
                 F   Dm
With his pointed shoes and his bells
F   Dm
Speaking to some French girl
B♭   C7
Who says she knows me well

cont.

          B♭   F
And I would send a message
     Dm   F
To find out if she's talked
      Dm   F
But the post office has been stolen
               B♭   F
And the mailbox box is locked

Chorus 2

Am
Oh, Mama, can this really be the end
          F   Fmaj7   Dm C
To be stuck inside of Mobile
               B♭   C7   F
With the Memphis blues again

Verse 3

F   Dm
Mona tried to tell me
     F   Dm
To stay away from the train line
       F   Dm
She said that all the railroad men
        B♭   C7
Just drink up your blood like wine
                   B♭   F
An' I said, "Oh, I didn't know that
                Dm   F
But then again, there's only one I've met
Dm   F
An' he just smoked my eyelids
B♭   F
An' punched my cigarette"

Chorus 3

Am
Oh, Mama, can this really be the end
          F   Fmaj7   Dm C
To be stuck inside of Mobile
               B♭   C7   F
With the Memphis blues again

Verse 4

F Dm
Grandpa died last week
F Dm
And now he's buried in the rocks
F Dm
But everybody still talks about
B♭ C7
How badly they were shocked
B♭ F
But me, I expected it to happen
Dm F
I knew he'd lost control
Dm F
When he built a fire on Main Street
B♭ F
And shot it full of holes

Chorus 4

Am
Oh, Mama, can this really be the end
F Fmaj7 Dm C
To be stuck inside of Mobile
B♭ C7 F
With the Memphis blues again

Verse 5

F Dm
Now the senator came down here
F Dm
Showing ev'ryone his gun
F Dm
Handing out free tickets
B♭ C7
To the wedding of his son
B♭ F
An' me, I nearly got busted
Dm F
An' wouldn't it be my luck
Dm F
To get caught without a ticket
B♭ F
And be discovered beneath a truck

```
                Am
Chorus 5        Oh, Mama, can this really be the end
                      F      Fmaj7  Dm C
                To be stuck inside of Mobile
                         B♭        C7    F
                With the Memphis blues again

                F                         Dm
Verse 6         Now the preacher looked so baffled
                       F                 Dm
                When I asked him why he dressed
                     F               Dm
                With twenty pounds of headlines
                B♭           C7
                Stapled to his chest
                      B♭               F
                But he cursed me when I proved it to him
                       Dm                            F
                Then I whispered, "Not even you can hide
                    Dm              F
                You see, you're just like me
                  B♭              F
                I hope you're satisfied"

                Am
Chorus 6        Oh, Mama, can this really be the end
                      F      Fmaj7  Dm C
                To be stuck inside of Mobile
                         B♭        C7    F
                With the Memphis blues again
```

```
              F                          Dm
Verse 7       Now the rainman gave me two cures
                    F                      Dm
              Then he said, "Jump right in"
                 F               Dm
              The one was Texas medicine
                 B♭                       C7
              The other was just railroad gin
                 B♭          F
              An' like a fool I mixed them
                   Dm                F
              An' it strangled up my mind
                     Dm                F
              An' now people just get uglier
                  B♭                 F
              An' I have no sense of time

              Am
Chorus 7      Oh, Mama, can this really be the end
                 F      Fmaj7   Dm C
              To be stuck inside of Mobile
                     B♭       C7     F
              With the Memphis blues again

              F                          Dm
Verse 8       When Ruthie says come see her
                 F                      Dm
              In her honky-tonk lagoon
                        F                          Dm
              Where I can watch her waltz for free
              B♭                        C7
              'Neath her Panamanian moon
              B♭                           F
              An' I say, "Aw come on now
                 Dm                                F
              You must know about my debutante"
                                Dm                              F
              An' she says, "Your debutante just knows what you need
                 B♭                       F
              But I know what you want"
```

```
             Am
Chorus 8     Oh, Mama, can this really be the end
                      F        Fmaj7    Dm C
             To be stuck inside of Mobile
                          B♭         C7     F
             With the Memphis blues again

             F                         Dm
Verse 9      Now the bricks lay on Grand Street
                            F                   Dm
             Where the neon madmen climb
                     F               Dm
             They all fall there so perfectly
               B♭                          C7
             It all seems so well timed
                 B♭                      F
             An' here I sit so patiently
             Dm                               F
             Waiting to find out what price
             Dm                      F
             You have to pay to get out of
             B♭                                   F
             Going though all these things twice

             Am
Chorus 9     Oh, Mama, can this really be the end
                      F        Fmaj7    Dm C
             To be stuck inside of Mobile
                          B♭         C7     F
             With the Memphis blues again

Outro        | F          | F        | F            | F        |

             | F  Em7♭5   | Dm7  C   | B♭  B♭(add9) | F        ||
```

SUBTERRANEAN HOMESICK BLUES

Words & Music by Bob Dylan

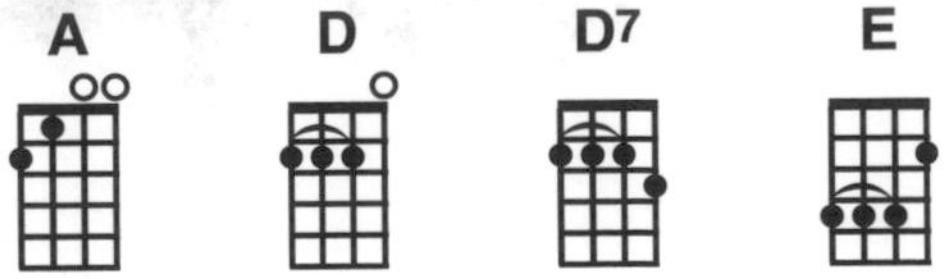

Intro | A | A | A D | A D | A D | A D ||

Verse 1

```
A                   D   A                  D
Johnny's in the basement mixing up the medicine
A              D    A                       D
I'm on the pavement thinking about the government
     A                 D    A               D
The man in the trench coat, badge out, laid off
A                   D       A
Says he's got a bad cough, wants to get it paid off
D7
Look out kid, it's somethin' you did
A                D         A
God knows when but you're doin' it again
    D     A                   D
You better duck down the alley way
A                 D
Lookin' for a new friend
    E
The man in the coon-skin cap by the big pen
        A                 D
Wants eleven dollar bills
A
You only got ten
```

Link 1 | A D | A D | A D | A D ||

Verse 2

```
A                        D    A                     D
Maggie comes fleet foot, face full of black soot
A                        D   A                    D
Talkin' that the heat put plants in the bed but
      A                     D    A                         D
The phone's tapped anyway. Maggie says that many say
       A                     D    A
They must bust in early May, orders from the D. A.
D7
Look out kid, don't matter what you did
A                   D    A              D
Walk on your tiptoes, don't try "No-Doz"
A                           D           A
Better stay away from those that carry around a fire hose
E
   Keep a clean nose, watch the plain clothes
     A                  D
You don't need a weatherman
     A
To know which way the wind blows
```

Link 2

| A D | A D | A D | A D ||

Verse 3

```
A                D    A                     D
Get sick, get well, hang around a ink well
A                    D     A                       D
Ring bell, hard to tell if anything is goin' to sell
A                D          A                D
Try hard, get barred, get back, write braille
A                     D   A
Get jailed, jump bail, join the army, if you fail
D7
Look out kid, you're gonna get hit
     A             D       A          D
But users, cheaters, six-time losers
A                          D
Hang around the theaters
E
Girl by the whirlpool lookin' for a new fool
A                      D
Don't follow leaders
A
Watch the parkin' meters
```

Link 3

| A D | A D | A D | A D ||

Verse 4

```
    A             D
Ah get born, keep warm
A             D      A
Short pants, romance, learn to dance
     D      A                D   A
Get dressed, get blessed, try to be a success
       D   A              D
Please her, please him, buy gifts
A
Don't steal, don't lift

Twenty years of schoolin'
D         A
And they put you on the day shift
D7
Look out kid, they keep it all hid
       A               D    A                 D
Better jump down a manhole, light yourself a candle
A              D   A
Don't wear sandals, try to avoid the scandals
E
   Don't wanna be a bum, you better chew gum
     A               D
The pump don't work
           A
'Cause the vandals took the handles
```

Coda

```
|: A   D   | A   D   :|
```
Repeat to fade

THE TIMES THEY ARE A-CHANGIN'

Words & Music by Bob Dylan

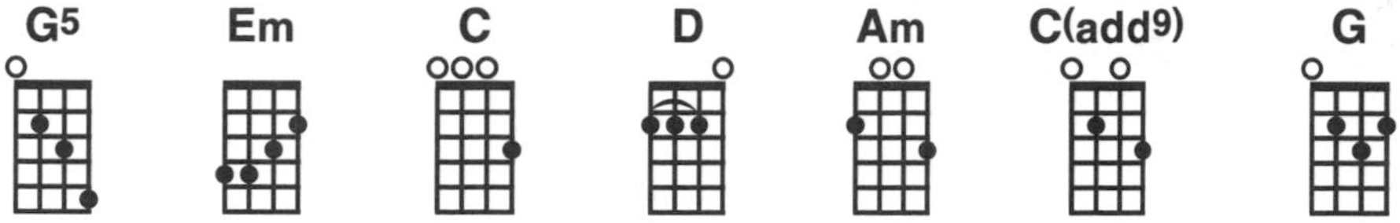

Verse 1

G5 Em C G5
Come gather 'round people wherever you roam

Em C D
And admit that the waters around you have grown

G5 Em C G5
And accept it that soon you'll be drenched to the bone

Am D
If your time to you is worth savin'

C(add9) G D
Then you better start swimmin' or you'll sink like a stone

G5 C G5
For the times they are a-changin'

Link 1

| G5 | Em C | G5 | G5 ||
(in')

Verse 2

G5 Em C G5
Come writers and critics who prophesize with your pen

Em C D
And keep your eyes wide the chance won't come again

G5 Em C G5
And don't speak too soon for the wheel's still in spin

Am D
And there's no tellin' who that it's namin'

C(add9) G D
For the loser now will be later to win

G5 C D G5
For the times they are a-changin'

Link 2 | G5 Em | C G5 | G5 D | C(add9) G | D | D ||
(in')

Verse 3

G5 Em C G5
Come senators, congressmen, please heed the call
Em C D
Don't stand in the doorway, don't block up the hall
G5 Em C G5
For he that gets hurt will be he who has stalled
Am D
There's a battle outside and it is ragin'
C(add9) G D
It'll soon shake your windows and rattle your walls
G5 C D G5
For the times they are a-changin'

Link 3 | G5 | D C(add9) | D G5 ||
(in')

Verse 4

G5 Em C G5
Come mothers and fathers throughout the land
Em C D
And don't criticize what you can't understand
G5 Em C G5
Your sons and your daughters are beyond your command
Am D
Your old road is rapidly agin'
C(add9) G D
Please get out of the new one if you can't lend your hand
G5 D G5
For the times they are a-changin'

Link 4 | G5 | Em C | G5 | D C(add9) |
(in')

| G D | D G5 | C D | G5 | G5 ||

Verse 5

```
G5          Em        C         G5
The line it is drawn, the curse it is cast
              Em       C       D
The slow one now will later be fast
       G5      Em        C       G5
As the present now will later be past
             Am      D
The order is rapidly fadin'
                    C(add9)   G       D
And the first one now will later be last
        G5    Em         D     G5
For the times they are a-changin'
```

Coda

```
| G5      | Em  C | G5      | Em  C    ||
(in')
```

TALKIN' BEAR MOUNTAIN PICNIC MASSACRE BLUES

Words & Music by Bob Dylan

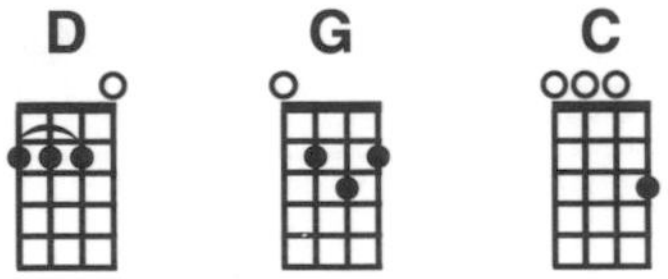

Intro | D | G ||

Verse 1

G C
Well, I saw it adver - tised one day
D
Bear Mountain picnic was comin' my way
G C
"Come along 'n' take a trip
D
We'll bring you up there on a ship
G
Bring the wife and kids
C D
Bring the whole family"

Yippee!

Link 1 | G | C | D | D |

| G | G ||

Verse 2

G   C
Well, I run right down ’n’ bought a ticket
                D
To this Bear Mountain Picnic
      G   C
But little did I rea - lize
                       D
I was in for a picnic surprise
       G
Had nothin’ to do with mountains
C   D
   I didn’t even come close to a bear

Link 2

As Link 1

Verse 3

G   C
Took the wife ’n’ kids down to the pier
D
Six thousand people there
           G   C
Every - body had a ticket for the trip
                 D   G
“Oh well,” I said, “It’s a pretty big ship
C   D
   Besides, anyway, the more the merrier”

Link 3

As Link 1

Verse 4

G   C
Well, we all got on ’n’ what d’ya think
        D
That big old boat started t’ sink
G   C
   More people kept a - pilin’ on
        D   G
That old ship was a-slowly goin’ down
C
   Funny way t’ start a picnic

Link 4

| D | D | G | G ||

```
            G                                C
*Verse 5*   Well, I soon lost track of m' kids 'n' wife
                          D
            So many people there I never saw in m' life
                         G                        C
            That old ship sinkin' down in the water
                            D
            There were six thousand people tryin' t' kill each other
            G                 C
              Dogs a-barkin', cats a-meowin'

            Women screamin', fists a-flyin', babies cryin'

            Cops a-comin', me a-runnin'
            D
              Maybe we just better call off the picnic
```

Link 5 As Link 1

```
            G                     C
*Verse 6*   I got shoved down 'n' pushed around
                          D
            All I could hear there was a screamin' sound
            G                        C
            Don't remember one thing more
                        D
            Just re - member wakin' up on a little shore
            G
              Head busted, stomach cracked
            D
            Feet splintered, I was bald, naked…

            Quite lucky to be alive though
```

Link 6 As Link 1

```
            G                        C
*Verse 7*   Feelin' like I climbed outa m' casket
              D
            I grabbed back hold of m' picnic basket
                         G              C
            Took the wife 'n' kids 'n' started home
                            D                       G
            Wishin' I'd never got up that morn
```

```
            G                      C
Verse 8     Now, I don't care just what you do
                         D
            If you wanta have a picnic, that's up t' you
                      G                         C
            But don't tell me about it, I don't wanta hear it
                                D                         G
            'Cause, see, I just lost all m' picnic spirit
            C                      D
               Stay in m' kitchen,    have m' own picnic…

            In the bathroom


Link 7      As Link 1


            G                         C
Verse 9     Now, it don't seem to me quite so funny
                 D
            What some people are gonna do f'r money
                      G                  C
            There's a bran' new gimmick every day
                    D                           G
            Just t' take somebody's money away
            C
              I think we oughta take some o' these people
            D
              And put 'em on a boat, send 'em up to Bear Mountain…

            For a picnic


Outro       | G     | C     | D     | D     |

            | G     | C     | D     | D     |

            | G     | G     ||
```

TANGLED UP IN BLUE

Words & Music by Bob Dylan

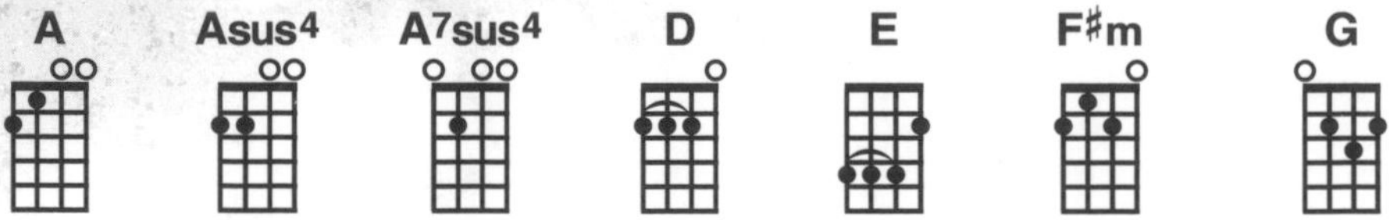

Intro | A Asus4 | A Asus4 | A Asus4 | A Asus4 ||

Verse 1

A A7sus4 A A7sus4
Early one mornin' the sun was shinin', I was layin' in bed

A A7sus4 D
Wond'rin' if she'd changed at all, if her hair was still red

A A7sus4 A A7sus4
Her folks they said our lives together sure was gonna be rough

A A7sus4
They never did like Mama's homemade dress

D
Papa's bankbook wasn't big enough

E F♯m A D
And I was standin' on the side of the road, rain fallin' on my shoes

E F♯m
Heading out for the East Coast

A D E
Lord knows I've paid some dues gettin' through

G D A Asus4
Tangled up in blue

| A Asus4 | A Asus4 | A Asus4 ||

Verse 2

A A7sus4 A A7sus4
She was married when we first met, soon to be divorced

A A7sus4 D
I helped her out of a jam, I guess, but I used a little too much force

A A7sus4 A A7sus4
We drove that car as far as we could, abandoned it out West

A A7sus4 D
Split up on a dark sad night both agreeing it was best

E F♯m A D
cont. She turned around to look at me as I was walkin' away

E F♯m
I heard her say over my shoulder

A D E
"We'll meet again someday on the avenue"

G D A Asus4
Tangled up in blue

| A Asus4 | A Asus4 | A Asus4 ||

A A7sus4 A A7sus4
Verse 3 I had a job in the great north woods working as a cook for a spell

A A7sus4 D
But I never did like it all that much and one day the ax just fell

A A7sus4 A A7sus4
So I drifted down to New Orleans where I happened to be employed

A A7sus4 D
Workin' for a while on a fishin' boat right outside of Delacroix

E F♯m A D
But all the while I was alone the past was close behind

E F♯m A D E
I seen a lot of women but she never escaped my mind, and I just grew

G D A Asus4
Tangled up in blue

| A Asus4 | A Asus4 | A Asus4 ||

A G/6A A A7sus4
Verse 4 She was workin' in a topless place and I stopped in for a beer

A A7sus4 D
I just kept lookin' at the side of her face in the spotlight so clear

A A7sus4
And later on as the crowd thinned out

A A7sus4
I's just about to do the same

A A7sus4
She was standing there in back of my chair

D
Said to me, "Don't I know your name?"

E F♯m
I muttered somethin' underneath my breath

A D
She studied the lines on my face

cont.

```
  E                      F♯m
I must admit I felt a little uneasy
             A                          D          E
When she bent down to tie the laces of my shoe
G          D     A     Asus4
Tangled up in blue

| A    Asus4 | A    Asus4 | A    Asus4 ||
```

Verse 5

```
A                     A7sus4             A                 A7sus4
She lit a burner on the stove and offered me a pipe
A                               A7sus4
"I thought you'd never say hello," she said
       D
"You look like the silent type"
             A                 A7sus4                A               A7sus4
Then she opened up a book of poems and handed it to me
A                  A7sus4                  D
Written by an Italian poet from the thirteenth century
      E                        F♯m
And every one of them words rang true
      A                          D
And glowed like burnin' coal
E                    F♯m
Pourin' off of every page
                A                 D                      E
Like it was written in my soul from me to you
G          D     A     Asus4
Tangled up in blue

| A    Asus4 | A    Asus4 | A    Asus4 ||
```

Verse 6

```
  A                           A7sus4
I lived with them on Montague Street
      A                           A7sus4
In a basement down the stairs
              A                     A7sus4
There was music in the cafés at night
            D
And revolution in the air
            A            A7sus4
Then he started into dealing with slaves
      A                              A7sus4
And something inside of him died
A                          A7sus4                D
She had to sell everything she owned and froze up inside
```

cont.

```
     E               F#m             A             D
And when finally the bottom fell out I became withdrawn
     E                F#m
The only thing I knew how to do
        A                D                 E
Was to keep on keepin' on like a bird that flew
G        D     A     Asus4
Tangled up in blue

| A    Asus4 | A    Asus4 | A    Asus4 ||
```

Verse 7

```
   A              A7sus4            A             A7sus4
So now I'm goin' back again, I got to get to her somehow
A                  A7sus4                      D
All the people we used to know they're an illusion to me now
A                   A7sus4 A                       A7sus4
Some are mathematicians, some are carpenters' wives
       A                    A7sus4
Don't know how it all got started
             D
I don't know what they're doin' with their lives
     E             F#m       A                  D
But me, I'm still on the road headin' for another joint
E              F#m
We always did feel the same
        A                     D       E
We just saw it from a different point of view
G        D     A    Asus4
Tangled up in blue

| A    Asus4 | A    Asus4 | A    Asus4 ||
```

Coda

```
|: A   A7sus4 | A   A7sus4 | A   A7sus4 | D         :|
|  E   F#m    | A   D      | E   F#m    | A   D      |
|  E          | G  D  A    ||
```

TEARS OF RAGE

Words & Music by Bob Dylan & Richard Manuel

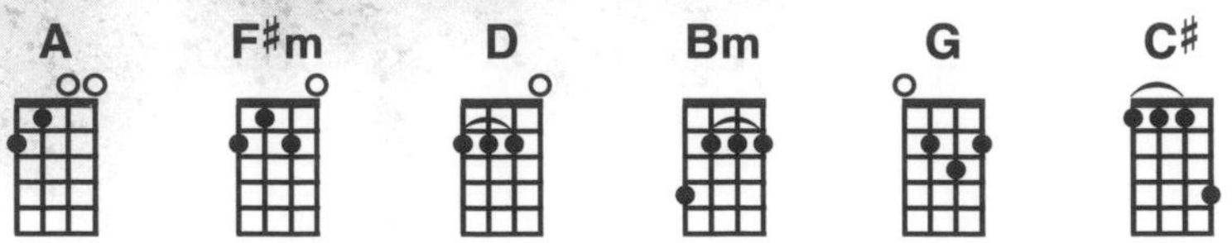

Verse 1

```
A                           F♯m
   We carried you in our arms
    D                  Bm
On Independence Day
A  G                         D
    And now you'd throw us all aside
    A
And   put us on our way
                                      F♯m
Oh what dear daughter 'neath the sun
         D                 Bm
Would    treat a father so
A     G                 D
   To   wait upon him hand and foot
   A
And always tell him, "No?"
```

Chorus 1

```
C♯                   F♯m
   Tears of rage,     tears of grief
D                       A
   Why must I always   be the thief?
C♯
   Come to me now, you know
        F♯m
We're     so alone
D       Bm    A
   And life is brief
```

Verse 2

```
A                           F♯m
We pointed out the way to go
      D                          Bm
And    scratched your name in sand
A  G                                D
   Though you just thought it was nothing more
        A
Than a place for you to stand
```

```
                                                        F♯m
cont.       Now, I want you to know that while we watched
                     D                            Bm
            You dis - cover there was no one true
            A      G         D
              Most   ev'rybody   really thought
                    A
            It was a childish thing to do

            C♯              F♯m
Chorus 2      Tears of rage,    tears of grief
            D                A
              Must I always   be the thief?
            C♯
              Come to me now, you know
                 F♯m
            We're     so low
            D       Bm   A
              And life is brief

            A                    F♯m
Verse 3     It was all very pain - less
                D                          Am
            When you went out to receive
            A G                    D
                All that false in - struction
                          A
            Which we never could believe
                                                F♯m
            And now the heart is filled with gold
            D                     Bm
              As if it was a purse
            A      G                   D
              But, oh, what kind of love is this
                      A
            Which goes from bad to worse?

Chorus 3    As Chorus 2
```

THINGS HAVE CHANGED

Words & Music by Bob Dylan

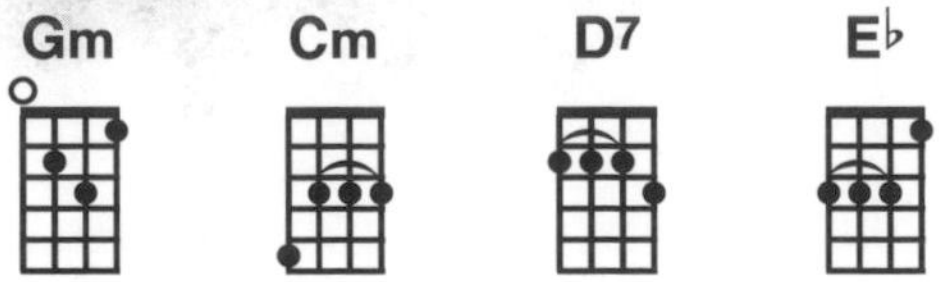

Intro | Gm | Gm | Gm | Gm ||

Verse 1
```
Gm
   A worried man with a worried mind
Cm
   No one in front of me and nothing behind
            Gm                                          D7
There's a woman on my lap and she's drinking champagne
Gm
   Got white skin, got assassin's eyes
Cm
   I'm looking up into the sapphire-tinted skies
     Gm                           D7  Gm
I'm well dressed, waiting on the last   train
```

Pre-chorus 1
```
E♭                                D7       Gm
Standing on the gallows with my head in a noose
     E♭                                        D7
Any minute now I'm expecting all hell to break  loose
```

Chorus 1
```
Gm
People are crazy and times are strange
     Cm
I'm locked in tight, I'm out of range
  Gm              D7          Gm
I used to care, but things have changed
```

Link 1 | Gm | Gm | Cm | Cm |

| Gm | Gm D7 | Gm | Gm ||

Verse 2

```
     Gm
This place ain't doing me any good
    Cm
I'm in the wrong town, I should be in Hollywood
    Gm                                           D7
Just for a second there I thought I saw something move
           Gm
Gonna take dancing lessons, do the jitterbug rag
     Cm
Ain't no shortcuts, gonna dress in drag
       Gm                              D7          Gm
Only a fool in here would think he's got anything to prove
```

Pre-chorus 2

```
E♭                                    D7      Gm
Lot of water under the bridge, lot of other stuff too
E♭                                       D7
Don't get up gentlemen, I'm only passing through
```

Chorus 2

```
Gm
People are crazy and times are strange
    Cm
I'm locked in tight, I'm out of range
  Gm              D7         Gm
I used to care, but things have changed
```

Link 2

```
| Gm        | Gm        | Cm        | Cm        |

| Gm        | Gm   D7   | Gm        | Gm        ||
```

Verse 3

```
         Gm
I've been walking forty miles of bad road
      Cm
If the Bible is right, the world will explode
          Gm                                       D7
I've been trying to get as far away from myself as I can
Gm
   Some things are too hot to touch
Cm
   The human mind can only stand so much
     Gm               D7     Gm
You can't win with a losing   hand
```

Pre-chorus 3

```
         E♭                          D7        Gm
Feel like falling in love with the first woman I meet
           E♭                                  D7
Putting her in a wheelbarrow and wheeling her down the street
```

Chorus 3

```
Gm
People are crazy and times are strange
  Cm
I'm locked in tight, I'm out of range
 Gm                   D7          Gm
I used to care, but things have changed
```

Link 3

| Gm | Gm | Cm | Cm |
| Gm | Gm D7 | Gm | Gm ||

Verse 4

```
 Gm
I hurt easy, I just don't show it
            Cm
You can hurt someone and not even know it
   Gm                                         D7
The next sixty seconds could be like an eternity
           Gm
Gonna get low down, gonna fly high
          Cm
All the truth in the world adds up to one big lie
         Gm                                   D7      Gm
I'm in love with a woman who don't even appeal to me
```

Pre-chorus 4

```
   E♭                               D7              Gm
Mr. Jinx and Miss Lucy, they  jumped in the lake
E♭                           D7
  I'm not that eager to make a mistake
```

Chorus 4

```
Gm
People are crazy and times are strange
  Cm
I'm locked in tight, I'm out of range
 Gm                   D7          Gm
I used to care, but things have changed
```

Coda

| Gm | Gm | Cm | Cm |
| Gm | Gm D7 || *To fade*

TRYING TO GET TO HEAVEN

Words & Music by Bob Dylan

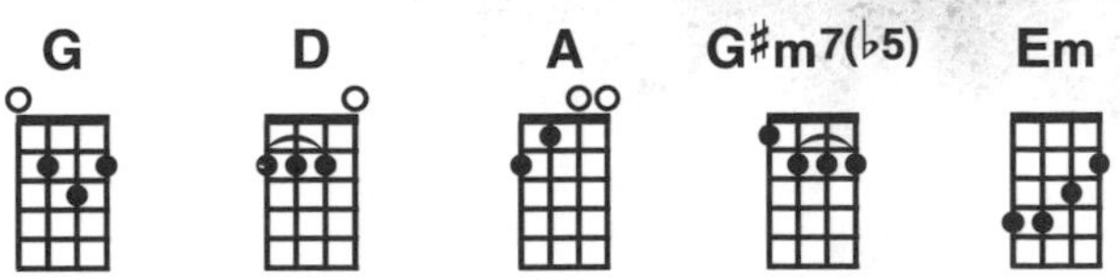

To match recording, tune ukulele up a semitone

Intro G D | A | A | D | D ‖

Verse 1

```
G                   A
    The air is getting hotter
G                        D
    There's a rumbling in the skies
G                                       A
I've been wading through the high muddy water
G                            D
    With the heat rising in my eyes
G♯m7(♭5)                           G
    Every day your memory grows dimmer
Em                           D
    It doesn't haunt me like it did before
G                                        A
    I've been walking through the middle of nowhere
G                                           D
    Trying to get to heaven before they close the door
```

Verse 2

```
G                        A
When I was in Mis - souri
G                         D
   They would not let me be
G                              A
   I had to leave there in a hurry
G                              D
   I only saw what they let me see
G♯m7(♭5)                            G
   You broke a heart that loved you
                 Em                           D
Now you can seal up the book and not write anymore
G                                         A
   I've been walking that lonesome valley
G                                         D
Trying to get to heaven before they close the door
```

Verse 3

```
G                   A
   People on the platforms
G                   D
   Waiting for the trains
G                              A
I can hear their hearts a - beatin'
G                                   D
Like pendulums swinging on chains
            G♯m7(♭5)            G
I tried to give you everything
             Em                  D
That your heart was longing for
G                                       A
   I'm just going down the road feeling bad
G                                         D
Trying to get to heaven before they close the door
```

Instrumental

```
| G        | A        | G        | D        |
| G        | A        | G        | D        |
| G♯m7(♭5) | G        | Em       | D        |
| G        | A        | G        | D        ||
```

Verse 4

```
    G                   A
I'm going down the river
G                   D
   Down to New Or - leans
     G                                  A
They tell me everything is gonna be all right
G                                      D
   But I don't know what "all right" even means
     G♯m7(♭5)                      G
I was riding in a buggy with Miss Mary-Jane
     Em                       D
Miss Mary-Jane got a house in Baltimore
G                        A
   I been all around the world, boys
          G                                      D
Now I'm trying to get to heaven before they close the door
```

Verse 5

```
G                          A
   Gonna sleep down in the parlor
G               D
   And relive my dreams
G                         A
   I'll close my eyes and I wonder
G                                  D
If everything is as hollow as it seems
G♯m7(♭5)                        G
   Some trains don't pull no gamblers
   Em                           D
No midnight ramblers like they did before
G                          A
   I been to Sugar Town, I shook the sugar down
          G                                      D
Now I'm trying to get to heaven before they close the door
```

Outro

```
| G         | A   | G   | D   |
| G         | A   | G   | D   |
| G♯m7(♭5)  | G   | Em  | D   |
| G         | A   | G   | D   ||
```

THIS WHEEL'S ON FIRE

Words by Bob Dylan
Music by Rick Danko

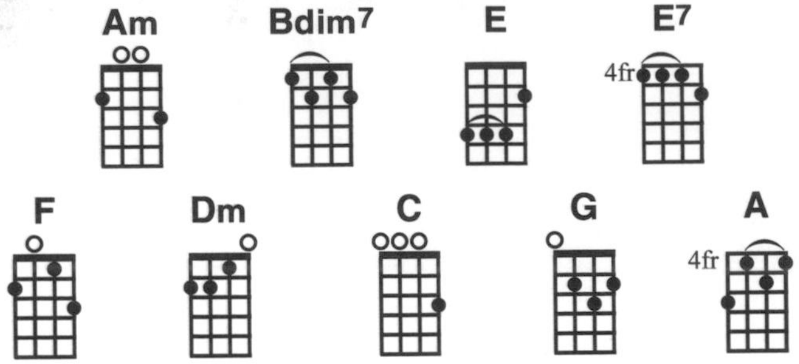

Intro | Am | Am ||

Verse 1

```
                Am
If your mem'ry serves you well
                 Bdim7
We were goin'   to meet again and wait
   E                      E7
So I'm goin' to unpack all my things
     F             Dm       Am
And sit before it gets too late
   C                 Am
No man alive will   come to you
     C                   Am
With another tale to tell
    C                        Am
But you know that we shall meet again
        F         Dm        Am
If your mem'ry serves you well
```

Chorus 1

```
Dm                F
   This wheel's on fire
C                 G
Rolling down the road
       C   G      F        C
Best notify my next of kin
F          G          A
This wheel shall explode!
```

Verse 2

```
        Am
If your mem'ry serves you well
            Bdim7
I was goin'  to confiscate your lace
     E              E7
And wrap it up in a sailor's knot
     F     Dm    Am
And hide it in your case
 C                   Am
If I knew for sure that it was yours…
          C           Am
But it was  oh so hard to tell
    C                          Am
But you knew that we would meet again
        F      Dm      Am
If your mem'ry serves you well
```

Chorus 2 As Chorus 1

Verse 3

```
        Am
If your mem'ry serves you well
         Bdim7
You'll remember you're the one
     E              E7
That called on me to call on them
   F             Dm   Am
To get you your favors done
    C       Am
And after ev'ry plan had failed
    C                        Am
And there was nothing more to tell
    C                   Am
You knew that we would meet again
        F      Dm      Am
If your mem'ry served you well
```

Chorus 3

```
Dm             F
   This wheel's on fire
C              G
Rolling down the road
      C  G    F    C
Best notify my next of kin
F        G      A
This wheel shall explode!
```

THUNDER ON THE MOUNTAIN

Words & Music by Bob Dylan

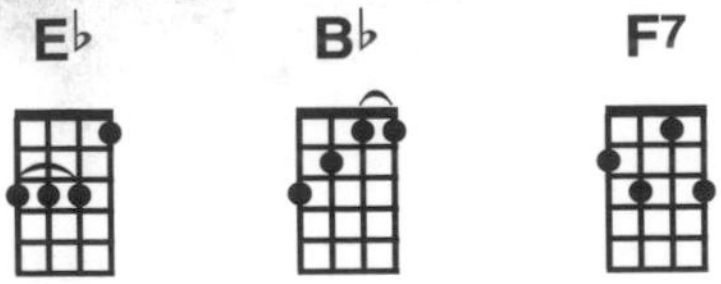

Intro

E♭	E♭	B♭	B♭
E♭	E♭	B♭	B♭
B♭	B♭	B♭	B♭	

Verse 1

B♭
Thunder on the mountain, fires on the moon

There's a ruckus in the alley and the sun will be here soon
E♭   B♭
Today's the day, gonna grab my trombone and blow
              F7   B♭
Well, there's hot stuff here and it's everywhere I go

Verse 2

B♭
I was thinkin' 'bout Alicia Keys, couldn't keep from crying

When she was born in Hell's Kitchen, I was living down the line
    E♭   B♭
I'm wondering where in the world Alicia Keys could be
        F7   B♭
I been looking for her even clear through Tennes - see

Verse 3

B♭
Feel like my soul is beginning to expand

Look into my heart and you will sort of understand
E♭   B♭
You brought me here, now you're trying to run me a - way
     F7   B♭
The writing's on the wall, come read it, come see what it say

```
Instrumental 1 | B♭   | B♭   | B♭   | B♭   |
               | E♭   | E♭   | B♭   | B♭   |
               | F7   | F7   | B♭   | B♭   ||
```

```
         B♭
Verse 4  Thunder on the mountain, rolling like a drum

         Gonna sleep over there, that's where the music coming from
                   E♭                                   B♭
         I don't need any guide, I already know the way
                F7                                            B♭
         Re - member this, I'm your servant both night and day
```

```
         B♭
Verse 5  The pistols are poppin' and the power is down

         I'd like to try somethin' but I'm so far from town
               E♭                                                   B♭
         The sun keeps shinin' and the North Wind keeps picking up speed
                             F7
         Gonna forget a - bout myself for a while,
                                                B♭
         Gonna go out and see what others need
```

```
         B♭
Verse 6  I've been sitting down studying the art of love

         I think it will fit me like a glove
                         E♭                            B♭
         I want some real good woman to do just what I say
                   F7                                                B♭
         Every - body got to wonder what's the matter with this cruel world today
```

```
Instrumental 2 | B♭   | B♭   | B♭   | B♭   |
               | E♭   | E♭   | B♭   | B♭   |
               | F7   | F7   | B♭   | B♭   ||
```

```
            B♭
Verse 7     Thunder on the mountain rolling to the ground

            gonna get up in the morning walk the hard road down
            E♭                                   B♭
            Some sweet day I'll stand beside my king
                         F7                          B♭
            I wouldn't be - tray your love or any other thing


            B♭
Verse 8     Gonna raise me an army, some tough sons of bitches

            I'll recruit my army from the orphanages
             E♭                                                B♭
            I been to St. Herman's church and I've said my religious vows
                F7                                B♭
            I've sucked the milk out of a thousand cows


            B♭
Verse 9     I got the porkchops, she got the pie

            She ain't no angel and neither am I
            E♭                                         B♭
            Shame on your greed, shame on your wicked schemes
            F7                                       B♭
            I'll say this, I don't give a damn about your dreams


Instrumental 3 | B♭      | B♭      | B♭      | B♭      |

               | E♭      | E♭      | B♭      | B♭      |

               | F7      | F7      | B♭      | B♭      ||


            B♭
Verse 10    Thunder on the mountain heavy as can be

            Mean old twister bearing down on me
                E♭                                           B♭
            All the ladies of Washington scrambling to get out of town
                             F7                                     B♭
            Looks like something bad gonna happen, better roll your airplane down
```

```
              B♭
*Verse 11*    Everybody's going and I want to go too

              Don't wanna take a chance with somebody new
                E♭                                        B♭
              I did all I could and I did it right there and then
                        F7                                      B♭
              I've al - ready confessed – no need to confess a - gain

              B♭
*Verse 12*    Gonna make a lot of money, gonna go up north

              I'll plant and I'll harvest what the earth brings forth
                  E♭                                         B♭
              The hammer's on the table, the pitchfork's on the shelf
                      F7                                           B♭
              For the love of God, you ought to take pity on your - self
```

Instrumental 4 | B♭ | B♭ | B♭ | B♭ |
| E♭ | E♭ | B♭ | B♭ |
| F7 | F7 | B♭ | B♭ ||

Outro | E♭ | E♭ | B♭ | B♭ ||

TOMORROW IS A LONG TIME

Words & Music by Bob Dylan

Intro

| E♭ B♭ E♭ B♭ | B♭ | E♭ B♭ |

| E♭ B♭ E♭ B♭ | B♭ ‖

Verse 1

```
B♭                          E♭           B♭            E♭
If today was not an endless highway
B♭                            E♭           B♭
If tonight was not a crooked trail
          E♭                 Fsus4        B♭           E♭      B♭
If to - morrow was - n't such a long time
         E♭                                  B♭                            E♭      B♭
Then lonesome would mean nothing to you at all
```

Chorus 1

```
              E♭                Fsus4                     B♭          E♭      B♭
Yes, and only if my own true love was waitin'
                              E♭          Fsus4              B♭               E♭      B♭
Yes, and if I could hear her heart a-softly poundin'
E♭          Fsus4               B♭          E♭      B♭
Only if she was lyin' by me
              E♭              D7/F♯                 B♭
Then I'd lie in my bed once again
```

| E♭ B♭ E♭ B♭ | E♭ B♭ ‖

Verse 2

```
B♭                           E♭                 B♭          E♭
I can't see my re - flection in the waters
                          E♭                        B♭     E♭      B♭
I can't speak the sounds that show no pain
           E♭              Fsus4            B♭          E♭      B♭
I can't hear the echo of my footsteps
                 E♭                                 B♭        E♭       B♭
Or can't remember the sound of my own name
```

Chorus 2

```
          E♭          Fsus4               B♭      E♭   B♭
Yes, and only if my own true love was waitin'
                     E♭        Fsus4         B♭       E♭     B♭
Yes, and if I could hear her heart a-softly poundin'
E♭     Fsus4         B♭     E♭   B♭
Only if she was lyin' by me
          E♭        F7              B♭
Then I'd lie in my bed once again

| E♭ B♭   E♭   | E♭ B♭   E♭   | B♭        ||
```

Verse 3

```
                         E♭             B♭    E♭    B♭
There's beauty in the silver, singin' river
                         E♭           B♭  E♭   B♭
There's beauty in the sunrise in the sky
              E♭                   Fsus4    E♭        B♭      E♭    B♭
But none of these and nothing else can   touch the beauty
      E♭         Fsus4     E♭         B♭    E♭   B♭
That I remember in my___ true love's eyes
```

Chorus 3

```
          E♭          Fsus4               B♭      E♭   B♭
Yes, and only if my own true love was waitin'
                     E♭        Fsus4         B♭       E♭     B♭
Yes, and if I could hear her heart a-softly poundin'
          E♭     Fsus4        B♭     E♭   B♭
Only if she was lyin' by me
          E♭        F7              B♭
Then I'd lie in my bed once again
```

Outro

```
| B♭   E♭   | B♭   F7   | B♭        ||
```

VISIONS OF JOHANNA

Words & Music by Bob Dylan

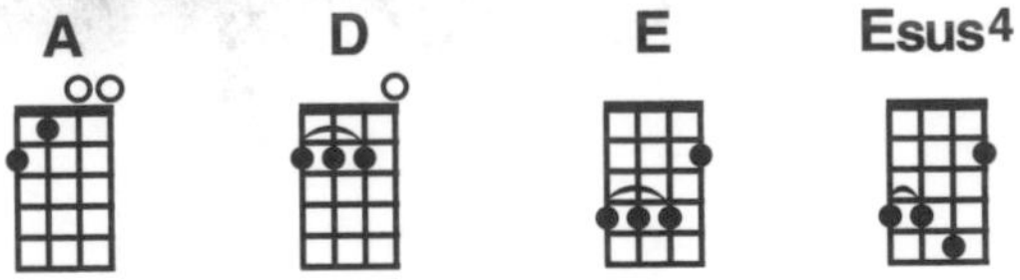


```
Intro    | A      | A      | D  E   | A  D   | A      ||

               A                        D
Verse 1  Ain't it just like the night to play  tricks
                   E               A      D  A
         When you're tryin' to be so quiet?
                                      D           E              A    D  A
         We sit here stranded, though we're all doin' our best to de - ny it
               E                                              A     D  A
         And Lou - ise holds a handful of rain, temptin' you to defy  it
                 D                        A
         Lights flicker from the opposite loft
            D                           A
         In this room the heat pipes just cough
             D                            A
         The country music station plays soft
                                                      E   Esus4  E
         But there's nothing, really nothing to turn off
                   A          D   E       A      D  A
         Just Lou - ise and her lover so en - twined
                   D                  A         E            A      D
         And these visions of Johanna     that conquer my mind

         | A      | D  E   | A  D   | A  D   ||
```

Verse 2

```
D             A
In the empty lot where the ladies
     D          E              A           D  A
Play blindman's bluff with the key chain
                             D                E
And the all-night girls they whisper of esca - pades
            A         D   A
Out on the "D" train
       E
We can hear the night watchman click his flashlight
                                                  A      D   A
Ask himself if it's him or them that's really in - sane
        D                               A
Louise, she's all right, she's just near
      D                           A
She's delicate and seems like the mirror
             D                                A
But she just makes it all too concise and too clear
                   E   Esus4  E
That Johanna's not here
    A
The ghost of 'lectricity
D            E             A      D  A
Howls in the bones of her face
            D                  A         E         A    D
Where these visions of Johanna   have now taken my place
```

| A | D E | A D | A D ||

Verse 3

```
D    A                   D                 E        A   D   A
Now, little boy lost, he takes himself so seriously
                           D             E           A   D   A
He brags of his misery, he likes to live dangerously
         E
And when bringing her name up
                                A   D   A
He speaks of a farewell kiss to me
     D                     A  D                     A
He's sure got a lotta gall  to be so useless and all
          D                  A                     E   Esus4 E
Muttering  small talk at the wall while I'm in the hall
```

cont.

A
How can I explain?

D E A D A
Oh, it's so hard to get on

D A E A D
And these visions of Johanna, they kept me up past the dawn

| A | D E | A D | A D ||

Verse 4

D A D E A D A
In - side the museums, Infinity goes up on trial

D A A D A
Voices echo this is what sal - vation must be like after a while

E
But Mona Lisa musta had the highway blues

A D A
You can tell by the way she smiles

D A
See the primitive wallflower freeze

D A
When the jelly-faced women all sneeze

D A
Hear the one with the mustache say, "Jeeze

E Esus4 E
I can't find my knees"

A D E A D A
Oh, jewels and binoculars hang from the head of the mule

D A E A D
But these visions of Johanna, they make it all seem so cruel

| A | D E | A D | A D ||

Verse 5

```
D     A                          D
The   peddler now speaks to the countess
              E         A          D   A
Who's pre - tending to care for him

Sayin', "Name me someone that's not a parasite
D               E          A                 D   A
   And I'll go out and say a prayer for him"
                E
But like Lou - ise always says

"Ya can't look at much, can ya man?"
                          A
As she, herself, pre - pares for him
          D                    A
And Ma - donna, she still has not showed
             D                  A
We see this empty cage now cor - rode
           D                            A
Where her cape of the stage once had flowed
             D                A
The fiddler, he now steps to the road
           D                               A
He writes ev'rything's been returned which was owed
        D                      A
On the back of the fish truck that loads
                          E
While my conscience ex - plodes
          A                D      E          A   D   A
The har - monicas play the skeleton keys and the rain
           D                A          E             A   D
And these visions of Johanna     are now all that remain
```

Outro

𝄆 A | D E | A D | A D 𝄇 *Repeat to fade*

WATCHING THE RIVER FLOW

Words & Music by Bob Dylan

Intro | C7 | Dm B♭ | F F7 B♭ B♭m | F C7 ||

Verse 1

F   B♭
What's the matter with me, I don't have much to say
F   G7   C7
Daylight sneakin' through the window and I'm still in this all-night café
F
Walkin' to and fro beneath the moon
                          B♭
Out to where the trucks are rollin' slow
   F   C7
To sit down on this bank of sand___
                    F   F7 B♭ B♭m F C7
And watch the river flow

Verse 2

F   B♭
Wish I was back in the city instead of this old bank of sand
         F   G7
With the sun beating down over the chimney tops
                                          C7
And the one I love so close at hand
F   B♭
If I had wings and I could fly,   I know where I would go
     F   C7
But right now I'll just sit here so con - tentedly
                    F   F7 B♭ B♭m F C7
And watch the river flow

Bridge 1

```
C7
   People disagreeing on all just about everything, yeah
F
Makes you stop and all wonder why
Dm                                         G7
Why only yesterday I saw some - body on the street
                       C7
Who just couldn't help but cry
     F
Oh, this ol' river keeps on rollin', though
B♭
No matter what gets in the way and which way the wind does blow
F                                    C7
And as long as it does I'll just sit here
                   F        F7  B♭  B♭m  F
And watch the river flow
```

Instrumental

```
| F      | F      | B♭          | B♭     |
| F      | G7     | C7          | C7     |
| F      | F      | B♭          | B♭     |
| F      | C7     | F  F7 B♭ B♭m | F     ||
```

Bridge 2

```
C7
People disagreeing everywhere you look
                         F
Makes you wanna stop and read a book
Dm                                                     G7
Why only yesterday I saw somebody on the street
            C7
That was really shook
     F
But this ol' river keeps on rollin', though
             B♭
No matter what gets in the way and which way the wind does blow
F                             C7
And as long as it does    I'll just sit here
                   F        F7  B♭  B♭m  F
And watch the river flow
```

Outro

```
Bb           F           Bb
Watch the river flow
               F          Bb
Watchin' the river flow
               F          Bb
Watchin' the river flow
           F                          C7
But I'll sit down on this bank of sand

And watch the river flow


| F    F7    Bb    Bbm  | F          ||
```

WHEN THE DEAL GOES DOWN

Words & Music by Bob Dylan

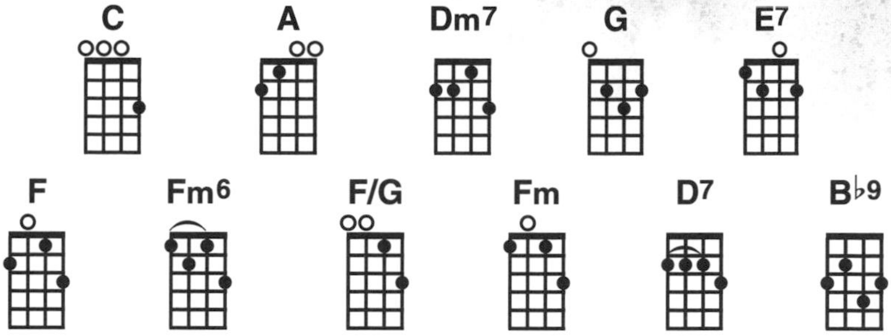

To match recording, tune ukulele up a semitone

Intro | C | A | Dm7 | G ||

Verse 1

```
(G)   C              E7              F                 Fm6
In the still of the night, in the world's ancient light
        C             F/G        C      G
Where wisdom grows up in strife
          C                 E7   F          Fm6
My be - wildering brain, toils in vain
             C                           F/G       C
Through the darkness on the path - ways of life
        F         Fm                  C
Each in - visible prayer is like a cloud in the air
     F                  C             D7     F/G
To - morrow keeps turning a - round
    C             E7         F             Fm6
We live and we die, we know not why
             C                       F/G       C       G
But I'll be with you when the deal goes down
```

Verse 2

```
(G) C            E7          F                  Fm6
We eat and we drink, we feel and we think
C                F/G        C      G
Far down the street we stray
  C             E7            F            Fm6
I laugh and I cry and I'm haunted by
          C                   F/G          C
Things I never meant nor wished to say
     F               Fm  C
The midnight rain     follows the train
     F             C              D7        F/G
We all wear the same thorny crown
C         E7          F            Fm6
Soul to soul, our shadows roll
             C                      F/G         C        G
And I'll be with you when the deal goes down
```

Guitar solo 1

C	E7	F	Fm6
C	F/G	C	G ‖

Verse 3

```
(G)  C            E7         F            Fm6
The moon gives light and shines by night
              C   F/G       C   F/G
I scarce - ly feel the glow
    C         E7       F               Fm6
We learn to live and then we for - give
          C           F/G       C
O'er the road we're bound to go
      F                Fm       C
More frailer than the flowers, these precious hours
      F           C           D7   F/G
That keep us so tightly bound
     C              E7          F                  Fm6
You come to my eyes like a vision from the skies
             C                      F/G         C        G
And I'll be with you when the deal goes down
```

```
Guitar solo 2  | C      | E7     | F      | B♭9    |

               | C      | F/G    | C      | G      ||

               (G) C              E7            F                     Fm6
Verse 4        I   picked up a rose and it poked through my clothes
                 C            F/G       C        G
               I followed the winding stream
                            C            E7    F                 Fm6
               I heard a deafening noise, I felt transient joys
               C                F/G              C
               I know they're not what they seem
                       F              Fm                       C
               In this earthly do - main, full of disap - pointment and pain
                            F    C       D7    F/G
               You'll ne - ver see me frown
                          C        E7              F          Fm6
               I owe my heart to you, and that's sayin' it true
                            C                     F/G         C         G
               And I'll be with you when the deal goes down


Outro          | C      | A      | Dm7    | Fm  G  | C      ||
```

WHAT GOOD AM I?

Words & Music by Bob Dylan

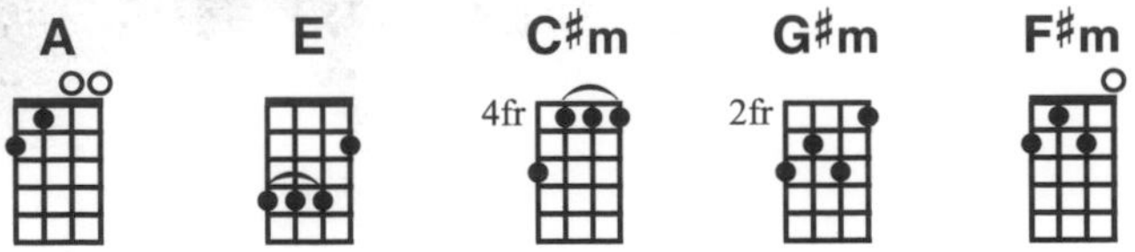


```
Intro    | A   E  | A   E  | A   E  ||

         E                     A          E  A  E
Verse 1    What good am I if I'm like all the rest
                             A             E
         If I turn away, when I see how you're dressed
            C♯m                            G♯m
         If I shut myself off so I can't hear you cry
         A   E   A   E   A  E
         What good am I?

         A          E   A            E    A   E
Verse 2  What good am I if I know and don't do
                                 A      E        A   E
         If I see and don't say, if I look right through you
            C♯m                        G♯m
         If I turn a deaf ear to the thunderin' sky
         A   E    A E    A  E
         What good am I?

                                 A        E       A E
Verse 3  What good am I while you softly weep
                                       A        E     A   E
         And I hear in my head what you say in your sleep
              C♯m                                  G♯m
         And I freeze in the moment like the rest who don't try
         A   E   A   E   A  E
         What good am I?
```

Bridge

```
          C#m
What good am I then to others and me
                                       G#m
If I've had every chance and yet still fail to see
          C#m
If my hands are tied must I not wonder within
                                    G#m              F#m
Who tied them and why and where must I have been?
```

Verse 4

```
E                        A          E        A    E
 What good am I if I say foolish things
                                 A          E    A    E
And I laugh in the face of what sorrow brings
        C#m                                     G#m
And I just turn my back while you silently die
A    E    A    E    A    E    A    E
What good am I?
```

Outro

```
|: E          | A     E | E          | A     E :|
| C#m         | G#m     |: A     E | A     E :|
```

Repeat to fade

WHEN I PAINT MY MASTERPIECE

Words & Music by Bob Dylan

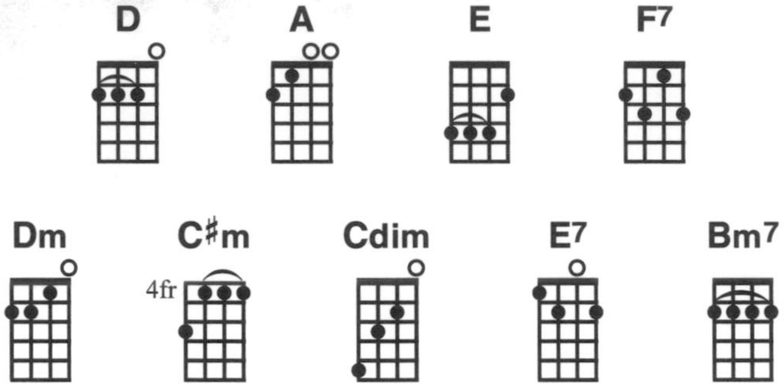

Intro D | A E | A D | A D ‖

Verse 1

```
A           D          A        D          A
   Oh, the streets of Rome are filled with rubble
D          A          E              A
Ancient footprints    are every - where
D          A                                 D      A
   You can almost think that you're seein' double
D      A          E                        A
On a cold, dark night on the Spanish Stairs
E                                  D      A
Got to hurry on back to my hotel room
                E                           D      A
Where I've got me a date with Botti - celli's niece
D      A                      D              A
   She promised that she'd be right there with me
D             A     E             A     D
   When I paint___ my master - piece
```

Link 1 | A D | A D ‖

Verse 2

(D) A D A
Oh, the hours I've spent inside the Coli - seum
D A E A
Dodging lions___ and wastin' time
D A D A
Oh, those mighty kings of the jungle, I could hardly stand to see 'em
D A E A
Yes, it sure has been a long, hard climb.
E D A
Train wheels runnin' through the back of my memory
E D A
When I ran on the hilltop following a pack of wild geese
D A D A
Someday, everything is gonna be smooth like a rhapsody
D A E A F7
When I paint my master - piece.

Bridge

Dm A
Sailin' round the world in a dirty gon - dola
C#m D E D A Cdim E7
Oh, to be back in the land of Coca-Cola!

Verse 3

A D A
I left Rome and landed in Brussels
D A E A
On a plane ride so bumpy that I almost cried
D A D A
Clergymen in uniform and young girls pul - lin' muscles
D A E A
Everyone was there to greet me when I stepped in - side
E D A
Newspapermen eat - ing candy
E D A
Had to be held down by big po - lice
D A D A
Someday, everything is gonna be diff'rent
D A E D A Bm7 A
When I paint my master - piece

WORKINGMAN'S BLUES #2

Words & Music by Bob Dylan

Intro | A | E | F♯m | A |

| D | A | Bm | E ||

Verse 1

(E) A E
There's an evenin' haze settlin' over town
F♯m A
Starlight by the edge of the creek
D A
The buyin' power of the prole - tariat's gone down
Bm E
Money's gettin' shallow and weak
A E
The place I love best is a sweet memory
F♯m A
It's a new path that we trod
D A
They say low wages are a reali - ty
Bm E
If we want to compete abroad

Verse 2

A E
My cruel weapons have been put on the shelf
F♯m A
Come sit down on my knee
D A
You are dearer to me than my - self
Bm E
As you yourself can see

cont.

A E
I'm listenin' to the steel rails hum
F♯m A
Got both eyes tight shut
D A
Just sitting here trying to keep the hunger from
Bm E
Creeping it's way into my gut

Chorus 1

D A
Meet me at the bottom, don't lag behind
D A
Bring me my boots and shoes
D A
You can hang back or fight your best on the front line
Bm E A
Sing a little bit of these workingman's blues

Verse 3

A E
Now, I'm sailin' on back, ready for the long haul
F♯m A
Tossed by the winds and the seas
D A
I'll drag 'em all down to hell and I'll stand 'em at the wall
Bm E
I'll sell 'em to their enemies
A E
I'm tryin' to feed my soul with thought
F♯m A
Gonna sleep off the rest of the day
D A
Some - times no one wants what we got
Bm E
Some - times you can't give it a - way

Verse 4

(E) A E
Now the place is ringed with countless foes
F♯m A
Some of them may be deaf and dumb
D A
No man, no woman knows
Bm E
The hour that sorrow will come

```
              A                E
cont.         In the dark I hear the night birds call
                   F#m                     A
              I can hear a lover's breath
                D                            A
              I sleep in the kitchen with my feet in the hall
              Bm                            E
              Sleep is like a temporary death


Chorus 2      As Chorus 1

              A                                    E
Verse 5       Well, they burned my barn, they stole my horse
              F#m                     A
              I can't save a dime
                D                              A
              I got to be careful, I don't want to be forced
                   Bm               E
              Into a life of continual crime
                    A                         E
              I can see for myself that the sun is sinking
              F#m                               A
              How I wish you were here to see
              D                       A
              Tell me now, am I wrong in thinking
                  Bm                E
              That you have forgotten me?

              (E)      A                                      E
Verse 6       Now they worry and they hurry and they fuss and they fret
                  F#m                          A
              They waste your nights and days
              D                     A
                 Them I will for - get
                           Bm                E
              But you I'll re - member always
                  A                     E
              Old memories of you to me have clung
                     F#m                  A
              You've wounded me with words
                    D                                  A
              Gonna have to straighten out your tongue
                    Bm                             E
              It's all true, everything you have heard
```

Chorus 3 As Chorus 1

Verse 7

```
A                    E
In you, my friend, I find no blame
F♯m                           A
Wanna look in my eyes, please do
D               A
   No one can ever claim
         Bm                  E
That I took up arms against you
        A                  E
All a - cross the peaceful sacred fields
F♯m                  A
   They will lay you low
        D                          A
They'll break your horns and slash you with steel
  Bm                   E
I say it so it must be so
```

Verse 8

```
(E)     A                       E
Now I'm down on my luck and I'm black and blue
      F♯m                                 A
Gonna give you another chance
    D                      A
I'm all alone and I'm ex - pecting you
   Bm                        E
To lead me off in a cheerful dance
        A                    E
I got a brand new suit and a brand new wife
F♯m                    A
I can live on rice and beans
D                          A
Some people never worked a day in their life
      Bm                  E
Don't know what work even means
```

Chorus 4 As Chorus 1

Outro

𝄆 A	E	F♯m	A	
D	A	Bm	E	𝄇 *Repeat and fade*

YOU AIN'T GOIN' NOWHERE

Words & Music by Bob Dylan

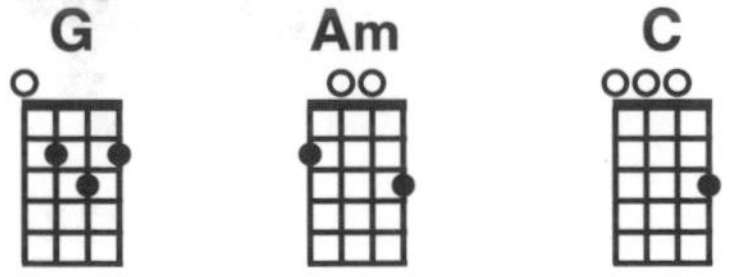

Intro ‖: G | G | G | G :‖

Verse 1

G Am
Clouds so swift, rain won't lift
C G
Gate won't close, railings froze
Am
Get your mind off wintertime
C G
You ain't goin' nowhere

Chorus 1

G Am
Whoo - ee! Ride me high
C G
Tomorrow's the day my bride's gonna come
G Am
Oh, oh, are we gonna fly
C G
Down in the easy chair!

Verse 2

G Am
I don't care how many letters they sent
G
Morning came and morning went
C Am
Pick up your money and pack up your tent
C G
You ain't goin' nowhere

Chorus 2 As Chorus 1

Verse 3

```
G                      Am
Buy me a flute and a gun that shoots
C                        G
Tailgates and substitutes
                      Am
Strap yourself to the tree with roots
C                        G
You ain't goin' nowhere
```

Chorus 3 As Chorus 1

Verse 4

```
G                   Am
Genghis Khan, he could not keep
C                            G
All his kings supplied with sleep
                         Am
We'll climb that hill no matter how steep
C                   G
When we get up to it
```

Chorus 4 As Chorus 1

Outro |: G | Am | C | G :| *Repeat to fade*

YOU'RE A BIG GIRL NOW

Words & Music by Bob Dylan

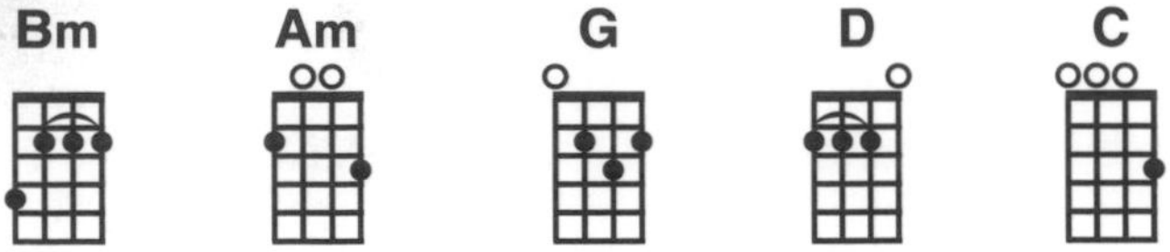

Intro

Bm	Am	Bm	Am
G D	C	G D	C
Am	Bm Am D	G	D	

Verse 1

Bm   Am
Our conversation   was short and sweet
Bm   Am
It nearly swept me   off-a my feet
              G   D C
And I'm back in the rain, oh, oh
                              G   D C
And you are on dry land
                                          Am
You made it there somehow
Bm   Am   D G D
You're a big girl now

Verse 2

Bm   Am
Bird on the horizon,   sittin' on a fence
Bm   Am
He's singin' his song for me   at his own expense
              G   D C
And I'm just like that bird, oh, oh
                              G   D C
Singin' just for you
                              Am
I hope that you can hear
Bm   Am   D   G D
Hear me singin' through these tears

Verse 3

```
Bm                         Am
   Time is a jet plane,     it moves too fast
Bm                                 Am
   Oh, but what a shame if all we've shared can't last
      G                     D  C
I can change, I swear, oh, oh
                            G      D C
See what you can do
                    Am
I can make it through
Bm     Am     D    G    D
   You    can make it too
```

Verse 4

```
Bm                         Am
   Love is so simple,     to quote a phrase
Bm                                            Am
   You've known it all the time, I'm learnin' it these days
      G                                D  C
Oh, I know where I can find you, oh, oh
                      G      D C
In somebody's room
                           Am
It's a price I have to pay
Bm          Am      D  G    D
   You're a big girl all the way
```

Verse 5

```
Bm                                Am
    A change in the weather     is known to be extreme
Bm                                           Am
   But what's the sense of changing horses in midstream?
          G                   D  C
I'm going out of my mind, oh, oh
                                G      D C
With a pain that stops and starts
                            Am
Like a corkscrew to my heart
Bm      Am          D       G     D
   Ever since we've been apart
```

Outro

```
| Bm      | Am          | Bm      | Am      |
| G   D   | C           | G  D    | C       |
| Am      | Bm  Am  D   | G       | D       | G        ‖ To fade
```

ALSO AVAILABLE FROM ALL GOOD MUSIC SHOPS...

AM1008271

AM1008282

AM995060

OP53251

AM950060

AM997304

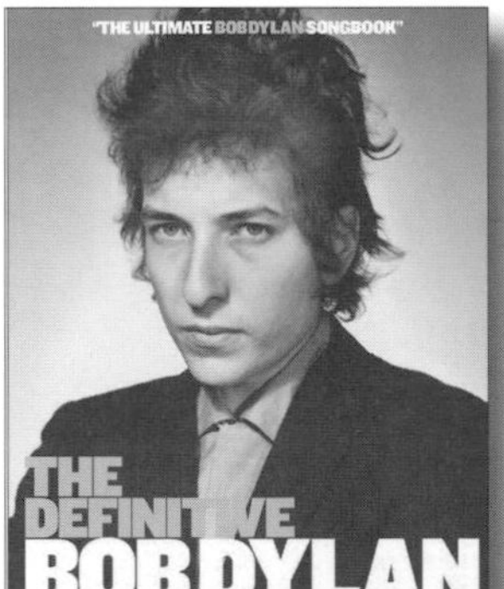

AM978923

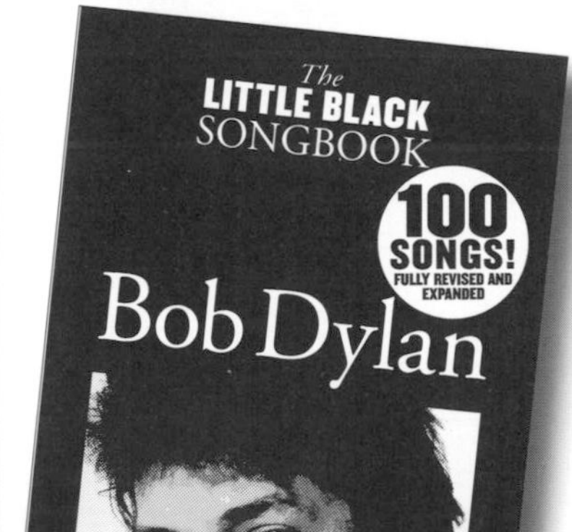

AM1007380

IN CASE OF DIFFICULTY PLEASE CONTACT:
MUSIC SALES LIMITED,
NEWMARKET ROAD, BURY ST EDMUNDS,
SUFFOLK, IP33 3YB, UK.
www.musicsales.com